2 B

SPECTRUM

A Communicative Course in English

Sandra Costinett
with *Donald R. H. Byrd*

Donald R. H. Byrd *Project Director*

Anna Veltfort *Art Director*

Longman

Library of Congress has cataloged the full edition of this title as follows:

Costinett, Sandra.
    Spectrum 2, a communicative course in English / Sandra Costinett
    with Donald R. H. Byrd; Donald R. H. Byrd, project director; Anna
    Veltfort, art director.
        p.   cm.
    Also published in a two-book split edition
    ISBN 0-13-829979-X
    1. English language--Textbooks for foreign speakers. I. Byrd,
    Donald R. H. II. Title. III. Title: Spectrum two.
    PE1128.W359 1993
    428.2'4--dc20   192-47370
                                                            CIP

    ISBN (2A) 0-13-829987-0   ISBN (2B) 0-13-830027-5

Project Manager: Nancy L. Leonhardt
Editorial Project Directors: Karen Davy and Larry Anger
Assistants to the Editors: Andrew Gitzy, Stephanie Karras, Sylvia P. Bloch

Production Manager: Sylvia Moore
Production Editor and Compositor: Jan Sivertsen
Technical Support and Assistance: Molly Pike Ricardi and David Ricardi
Pre-Press Buyer and Scheduler: Ray Keating
Manufacturing Buyer: Lori Bulwin

Cover Design: Roberto de Vicq
Interior Concept and Page-by-Page Design: Anna Veltfort
©1993 by Prentice Hall Regents

A Pearson Education Company
Pearson Education
10 Bank Street
White Plains, NY 10606

Printed in the United States of America
10 9

ISBN 0-13-830027-5

INTRODUCTION

Spectrum 2A and 2B represent the second level of a six-level course designed for adolescent and adult learners of English. The student book, workbook, and audio program for each level provide practice in all four communication skills, with a special focus on listening and speaking. Levels 1 and 2 are appropriate for beginning students and "false" beginners. Levels 3 and 4 are intended for intermediate classes, and 5 and 6 for advanced learners of English. The first four levels are offered in split editions — 1A, 1B, 2A, 2B, 3A, 3B, 4A, and 4B. The student books and workbooks for levels 1 to 4 are also available in full editions.

Spectrum is a "communicative" course in English, based on the idea that communication is not merely an end-product of language study, but rather the very process through which a new language is acquired. *Spectrum* involves students in this process from the very beginning by providing them with useful, natural English along with opportunities to discuss topics of personal interest and to communicate their own thoughts, feelings, and ideas.

In *Spectrum*, understanding a new language is considered the starting point for communication. The student books thus emphasize the importance of comprehension, both as a useful skill and as a natural means of acquiring a language. Students begin each unit by listening to and reading conversations that provide rich input for language learning. Accompanying activities enhance comprehension and give students time to absorb new vocabulary and structures. Throughout the unit students encounter readings and dialogues containing structures and expressions not formally introduced until later units or levels. The goal is to provide students with a continuous stream of input that challenges their current knowledge of English, thereby allowing them to progress naturally to a higher level of competence.

Spectrum emphasizes interaction as another vital step in language acquisition. Interaction begins with simple communication tasks that motivate students to use the same structure a number of times as they exchange real information about themselves and other topics. This focused practice builds confidence and fluency and prepares students for more open-ended activities involving role playing, discussion, and problem solving. These activities give students control of the interaction and enable them to develop strategies for expressing themselves and negotiating meaning in an English-speaking environment.

The *Spectrum* syllabus is organized around functions and structures practiced in thematic lessons. Both functions and structures are carefully graded according to simplicity and usefulness. Structures are presented in clear paradigms with informative usage notes. Thematic lessons provide interesting topics for interaction and a meaningful vehicle for introducing vocabulary.

Student Book 2B consists of seven units, each divided into one- and two-page lessons. The first lesson in each unit presents a series of authentic conversations, providing input for comprehension and language acquisition. A preview activity prepares students to understand the cultural material in the conversations. New functions and structures are then practiced through interactive tasks in several thematic lessons. A two-page, fully illustrated comprehension lesson provides further input in the form of a dialogue, pronunciation activity, and listening exercise all related to the storyline for the level. This lesson includes a role-playing activity as well. The final lesson of the unit presents authentic documents such as historical texts and news articles for reading comprehension practice. Review lessons follow units 1 to 4 and units 5 to 7.

Workbook 2B is carefully coordinated with the student book. Workbook lessons provide listening and writing practice on the functions, structures, and vocabulary introduced in the corresponding student book lessons. Units end with a guided composition related to the theme of the reading in the student book.

Audio Program 2B offers two cassettes for the student book with all conversations, model dialogues, listening activities, and readings dramatized by professional actors in realistic recordings with music and sound effects. A third cassette includes the workbook listening activities.

Teacher's Edition 2B features full-sized reproductions of each student-book page with teaching suggestions, listening scripts, and answer keys on the facing page. Listening scripts and answer keys for the workbook appear in the appendix.

A **Testing Package** includes a placement test as well as midterm and final tests for each level.

UNIT	PAGES	THEMES	FUNCTIONS
1 Lessons 1 – 6	1–12	Moods and feelings Suggestions Opinions Plans	Talk about moods and feelings Suggest a possible activity Accept or reject a suggestion Ask for and give opinions Talk about plans
2 Lessons 7 – 11	13–22	Accidents Recommendations Emergencies Explanations Past activities	Find out what's wrong Make a recommendation Call for help Report an emergency Explain what happened Talk about past activities
3 Lessons 12 – 17	23–32	Offers Problems Suggestions Telephone calls	Get to know someone Keep a conversation going Talk about abilities Give someone a message Instruct someone politely Get the correct change
4 Lessons 18 – 23	33–42	Plans Directions Job interviews School Skills and interests	Talk about plans Wish someone well Ask for and give directions Thank someone Interview for a job Talk about school Talk about skills and interests

S E Q U E N C E

LANGUAGE	FORMS	SKILLS
Review	Review	Review
Let's go to a baseball game. Why don't we go to a soccer game instead? I like soccer better than baseball. The train is faster than the bus. Soccer is more exciting than baseball. Baseball is less exciting than soccer. The Grand Hotel isn't as expensive as the Ritz. Should we take some food with us? Yes. It's more expensive at the stadium. What's the weather going to be like on Saturday? It's supposed to get colder. It's going to be cloudy too. What does your father look like? He's a little taller than I am. He's got curly brown hair, and he wears glasses. And what's he like? He's sort of quiet, but he's very nice.	Comparisons with *...er than,* *more/less ... than,* and *as ... as* *Should* *Be supposed to* *Look like* *Be like*	Listen for preferences Listen to a weather report Listen to the intonation of affirmative statements with contrast Read a magazine article Write a letter (workbook)
May I use your phone? Certainly. I lost my passport. Do you have any identification? Yes. Here's a credit card. Thank you very much. Don't mention it. Just be more careful next time. What happened exactly? A car went through the red light. I slammed on the brakes and went off the road. Can you describe the other car? I think it was a Ford Escort. What color was it? Dark blue. Did you get the license plate number? No, I didn't. Yes. It was XYZ 93M. I'm sorry (that) you wrecked your car. I hope (that) your car is O.K. I think (that) you're very lucky. Who has had an accident? I have. What happened? I was on my bike and a car hit me.	*May* *That* + noun clause Review: subject questions and short answers	Listen to descriptions of car accidents Listen to the intonation of statements and questions Read a short magazine article Write an accident report (workbook)
What are you doing this weekend? I'm not sure yet. Why? I think I'll have some people over for dinner. My parents are having a barbecue on Sunday. Would you like to come? O.K. That sounds nice. Can I bring anything? Oh, no. We already have everything we need. I could bring something to drink. Well, if you want to, but you really don't have to. Would you like some help with that? Oh, thanks. No, thanks. I can manage. You're Rick's friend, aren't you? Yes, I am. I'm Tracy, Rick's sister. So, how do you know Rick? We go to school together. Carol works at ABC Industries. So does Tracy. Carol isn't going to school full time. Neither is Tracy. You're not leaving already, are you? Yes. I have to go. But I want to thank you for everything. Well, I'm glad you could come. So am I. I enjoyed myself very much.	Review: the future with *going to*, the present continuous as future, and the future with *will* Tag questions Rejoinders with *so* and *neither*	Listen for people's plans Listen for things people have in common Listen to the intonation of statements and questions Read a survey Write about plans (workbook)
Review	Review	Review

Who's Who in Spectrum 2B:

Steve Kovacs owns an auto repair shop in Los Angeles, California. He has a lot of bills to pay, so he decides to advertise his shop on the radio.

Bob, a mechanic at Steve's repair shop, and Margaret, the bookkeeper, help Steve with the ad.

Charles (Charley) Jackson, a friend of Steve's, works in a bank. Once a week, Steve and Charley play on a soccer team after work.

Eva is Steve's younger sister. She's a high school student, and she's interested in photography. Eva needs a new camera, so she's looking for a part-time job.

Eva and Steve's mother, Emma, is a doctor. Their father died five years ago. Steve, who has his own apartment, often stops by to say hello to his mother and sister.

One evening Emma tells Steve and Eva that she met someone interesting a few days before: Tom Anderson, an airline pilot who just moved into the building.

PREVIEW

FUNCTIONS/THEMES	LANGUAGE	FORMS
Talk about moods and feelings	You're in a good mood today! Yeah. I just got some good news. You look upset. Is anything wrong? I'm just in a bad mood. I always get nervous when I have to take a test.	*Just* for the recent past Clauses with *when, as soon as, before,* and *after*
Suggest a possible activity Accept or reject a suggestion	Why don't we do something? Maybe we could go to a movie. That's a good idea. No. I don't feel like going anywhere. I'm not in the mood.	*Could* Indefinite compounds: *something, anything, nothing,* etc.
Ask for and give opinions	What did you think of the movie? I liked it a lot. I didn't enjoy it at all.	Review: the simple past tense
Talk about plans	What are you doing tonight? I'm having a party.	The present continuous as future

Preview the conversations.

Many things can put you in a good mood—for example, passing a test, meeting a good friend, or seeing a wonderful movie. What puts you in a good mood?

Some things that put people in a bad mood are failing a test, feeling sick, and not having enough money. What puts you in a bad mood or makes you feel depressed?

Unit 1 **1**

1. Moods and feelings

 Janet and Gary are close friends. They talk about why they feel good or feel depressed.

A

Janet You look upset. Is anything wrong?

Gary Oh, I'm just in a bad mood today.

Janet Why?

Gary I think I failed my math test.

Janet Oh, you probably passed.

Gary Well, maybe, but I always get nervous when I have to take a test.

Janet A lot of people do. But don't worry about it. You always do well in math.

B

Janet You're in a good mood today!

Gary Yeah. I just got some good news. We got our math tests back this morning.

Janet And?

Gary I didn't fail after all. In fact, I only made one mistake.

Janet That's great!

Gary Yeah. Hey, you look pretty happy today, too.

Janet I am! Exams are over and I'm having a party tonight. I hope you're still going to come.

Gary Of course. It sounds like fun. Can I bring anything?

Janet No, nothing. Everyone's coming around 8:00.

Gary O.K. See you then.

C

Gary You look tired.

Janet Oh, I just feel a little depressed. I always feel that way on Sunday afternoons.

Gary Really? Why?

Janet Because the weekend's almost over.

Gary Well, why don't we do something? Maybe we could go to a movie.

Janet No. I don't feel like going anywhere. I'm not in the mood.

Gary Come on, you need to get out of here. Me too. *Lucky in Love* is playing at the Baronet. Why don't we go see it?

Janet It is? Well, . . . O.K. Maybe you're right.

D

Janet What did you think of the movie?

Gary I didn't like it at all.

Janet Really? Why not?

Gary I don't know. I just didn't think it was very funny. How did you like it?

Janet I liked it a lot. It really put me in a good mood.

Figure it out

1. Listen and choose *a* or *b* to complete the sentences.

1. At first Gary thinks he failed his math test, so
   a. he is in a good mood.
   b. he is in a bad mood.

2. The next day Gary is in a good mood because
   a. he passed his math test.
   b. he's going to Janet's party.

3. On Sunday Janet is in a bad mood because
   a. the weekend is almost over.
   b. she hates to study.

4. Later Janet is in a good mood because
   a. she enjoyed the movie.
   b. the weekend is almost over.

2. Listen again and match.

1. You look upset. What's wrong?   h
2. I always get nervous when I have to take a test. g
3. You're in a good mood!   c
4. Can I bring anything?   e
5. Why don't we do something? a
6. You need to get out of here. b
7. What did you think of the movie? d
8. Why not?   f

a. No, I don't feel like going anywhere.
b. Maybe you're right.
c. Yeah. I just got some good news.
d. I didn't like it at all.
e. No, nothing.
f. I just didn't think it was very funny.
g. A lot of people do.
h. Oh, I'm just in a bad mood.

2. You look upset.

1 ▶ The people in the pictures are in a bad mood. Make a comment to complete each exchange. Use the words in the box. In some of the exchanges, there is more than one possible comment.
▶ Listen to the possible exchanges.

a. depressed	c. scared	e. tired
b. nervous	d. angry	f. bored

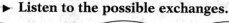

Picture 1: You look _____. / I just got some bad news.

Picture 2: You look _____. / I know. I stayed up late last night.

Picture 3: You look _____. / I am. I don't have anything to do.

Picture 4: You look _____. / I always get nervous when I fly.

Picture 5: You look _____. / I always get scared when I'm home alone.

Picture 6: You look _____. / I am! I had a two o'clock appointment, but my doctor didn't see me until four thirty!

2 ▶ Listen to the conversation.
▶ Imagine you are one of the people in exercise 1. Practice similar conversations with a partner.

A You look upset. Is anything wrong?
B Oh, I'm just in a bad mood.
A Why?
B I think I failed my math test.
A Oh, you probably passed.
B Well, maybe. I always get nervous when I have to take a test.
A A lot of people do.

I always get . . .	
nervous	before I take a trip.
scared	when I fly.
angry	when someone is late.
depressed	after I read the newspaper.
upset	when I fail a test.

3 ▶ Listen to the conversation.
▶ Imagine something put you in a good mood. Have a similar conversation with a partner.

A You're in a good mood today!
B Yeah. I just got some good news. I passed my math test.
A That's great!

Some things that put people in a good mood
I passed my exam.
I just got a check from my father.
I just moved into my new apartment.
I started my new job today.
I'm having a party tonight.

With the past tense, *just* often means "very recently."
I **just** got some good news.
I **just** moved into my new apartment.
I was **just** there.

With all tenses, *just* can also mean "only."
I **just** had toast for breakfast. Nothing else.
I **just** have two dollars.
I'm **just** going to study English tonight.

4 ▶ **Study the frame.**

Clauses with *when, as soon as, before,* and *after*		
I always get upset	**when**	I fail a test.
They have dinner	**as soon as**	they get home.
She studies hard	**before**	she takes a test.
He goes to class	**after**	he finishes work.

You can also say:

When I fail a test, I always get upset.
As soon as they get home, they have dinner.
Before she takes a test, she studies hard.
After he finishes work, he goes to class.

Notice the comma in these sentences.

5 ▶ **A woman wrote a letter to a radio show called "Tell Us Your Problem." Complete this paragraph from her letter with *when, before, after,* and *as soon as.* There may be more than one possibility for some items.**

present continuing

I'm always in a bad mood _____ when _____ I'm getting ready for a business trip. It's not too bad _____ after when _____ I drive or take a train. However, I get nervous _____ when _____ I have to fly. _____ After When _____ I get on a plane, I hold the arms of my seat so tight that my hands turn white. _____ When _____ the flight attendant offers something to drink or eat, I refuse. I'm afraid I'll get sick. And I can't even talk _____ before when _____ someone tries to strike up a conversation. _____ After When / as soon as _____ the plane lands, I feel much better. *begin* And I'm usually very hungry. So, _____ After When / as soon as _____ I get off, I go to the airport cafeteria. Finally, I get something to eat and relax!

6 ▶ **Now listen to the advice from the host of "Tell Us Your Problem." Then choose *a* or *b* to complete each statement.**

1. The host of "Tell Us Your Problem" agrees that
   a. a lot of people don't like to fly.
   b. most people like to fly.

2. The host suggests that passengers think about
   a. the positive things about flying.
   b. the negative things about flying.

3. The host says
   a. there are more automobile accidents than airplane accidents.
   b. there are more airplane accidents than automobile accidents.

4. He suggests
   a. holding your seat tight and not eating.
   b. reading a good book or taking a nap. *short sleep*

5. If absolutely necessary, he suggests
   a. staying home.
   b. getting a prescription from a doctor.

7 ▶ **Talk with your classmates. Tell them what puts you in a good or bad mood. Your classmates will offer advice.**

3. Why don't we do something?

1 ▶ **Listen to the two possible conversations.**
   ▶ **Have a similar conversation with a partner.**

A You look tired.
B Oh, I just feel a little depressed. I always feel that way on Sunday afternoons.
A Really? Why?
B Because the weekend's almost over.
A Well, why don't we do something? Maybe we could go to a movie.

B That's a good idea.   B No. I don't feel like going anywhere. I'm not in the mood.

Some possible activities
Maybe we could . . .
go to a movie.
go out for dinner.
go for a walk.
go for a drive.

2 ▶ **Study the frames: Indefinite compounds**

Affirmative statements	Negative statements
Let's do **something**.	I don't feel like doing **anything**.
Let's go **somewhere**.	I don't feel like going **anywhere**.
Let's invite **someone** over.	I don't feel like seeing **anyone**.

Yes-no questions	Negative short answers
Do you want to do **anything**?	No, **nothing**.
Do you want to go **anywhere**?	No, **nowhere**.
Do you want to invite **anyone** over?	No, **no one**.

someone = somebody
anyone = anybody
no one = nobody

I don't feel like seeing anybody.

You can also use *something, somewhere,* and *someone* in questions.

Do you want to do something?

3 ▶ **Complete the movie reviews with appropriate indefinite compounds.**

A Summer Holiday

Elliot doesn't feel like seeing ~~anybody~~ anyone after his wife leaves him. He just wants to go somewhere and be alone. But in Hawaii he meets Sarah, someone/somebody new and exciting. He doesn't know anything about Sarah, but he thinks she's hiding something from her past. Two strangers find romance in this mysterious love story.

SPACE MONSTERS

Strange monsters from somewhere in the galaxy invade the planet Xenon. King Astro can think of no one/nobody or nothing to stop them. Queen Larena might know someone/something that can help, but she's afraid to tell anyone about their problem. Can the scientist Dr. Strom help them before something terrible happens? This science fiction adventure is out of this world!

ASK FOR AND GIVE OPINIONS • REVIEW: THE SIMPLE PAST TENSE

 4
▶ **Listen to the movie review. Check (√) the things the film critic liked about the movie.**
▶ **Which movie did the critic see, *A Summer Holiday* or *Space Monsters*?**

_____ the acting   _____ the costumes   _____ the makeup
_____ the story   _____ the special effects   _____ the music

 5
▶ **Listen to the two possible conversations.**
▶ **Have a similar conversation with a partner.**

A What did you think of the movie?

B I didn't like it at all.

A Really? Why not?

B I don't know. I just didn't think it was very funny. How did you like it?

A I liked it a lot.

B I liked it a lot. The story was fascinating. How did you like it?

A I didn't enjoy it at all.

> **Some reasons**
>
> The story was fascinating.
> It showed a whole different way of life.
> The acting was excellent.
> The music was wonderful.
> I loved the food.
> The story was terrible.
> I didn't learn anything new.
> It wasn't very interesting.
> It lasted too long.
> The service was awful.

the restaurant

the book

the movie

the concert

6
▶ **Study the frame: The simple past tense**

Information questions				Affirmative statements			Negative statements			
How	did	you she they	like the movie?	I She They	**thought**	it was very good.	I She They	didn't	**think**	it was very good.
					enjoyed	it a lot.			**enjoy**	it at all.

 7
▶ **What did Mark and Sue think of *A Summer Holiday*?**
Complete their conversation. Use the words in parentheses.
▶ **Listen to check your work.**

Mark So, _where did you go_ (where/you/go) last night?
Sue _I went_ (I/go) to see *A Summer Holiday*.
Mark Oh, _I saw_ (I/see) that last week. _How did you like_ (how/you/like) it?
Sue _I enjoyed_ (I/enjoy) it a lot. The scenery was spectacular.
Mark Hmmm. Hawaii is beautiful. But _____ (what/you/think) of the acting?
Sue It was O.K. except for Marie Mansfield. I mean, _____ (she/not act). _she didn't act (well)_ _she just looked_ (she/just/look) pretty.
Mark Yeah, _I didn't think_ (I/not think) her acting was very good at all. _How did you like_ (how/you/like) the music?
Sue Well, _I thought_ (I/think) it was a little loud, but _it put_ (it/put) me in a good mood.

8
▶ **Talk to your classmates. Tell them about a movie or TV show you saw, or a book you read recently. Tell why you liked or didn't like it.**

4. You look pretty happy today.

 1 ▶ **What are these people thinking? Match the thoughts in the box with the pictures.**
▶ **Listen to check your work.**

a. I'm going on vacation tomorrow.
b. We're moving into our new apartment this weekend.
c. I'm getting married next week.

d. I'm starting a new job on Monday.
e. I'm having a party tonight.
f. I'm leaving work early today.

 2 ▶ **Listen to the conversation.**
▶ **Work with a partner. Practice similar conversations using the information in exercise 1 or your own good news.**

A You look pretty happy today.
B I am. I'm having a party tonight.
A That sounds like fun.

Some responses	
That's great!	That's really good news.
How exciting!	I'm really happy for you.
That sounds like fun.	Lucky you!

3 ▶ **Listen to the four conversations. Then match the two parts of the sentences.**

1. Melanie is   a. having dinner in a Chinese restaurant.
2. Sally and Tim are   b. moving to Hawaii.
3. Jack is   c. getting ready for a trip.
4. The Carvers are   d. coming home on Friday.

4 ▶ **Study the frame.**

Present continuous as future	You can often use the present continuous to talk about plans and intentions.
What **are** you **doing** tonight? I**'m having** a party.	*What are you doing tonight?* means *What are you going to do tonight?* *I'm having a party.* means *I'm going to have a party.*

 5 ▶ **Complete the four conversations, using the present continuous as future and the verbs in parentheses.**
▶ **Listen to check your work.**

Hey, Melanie, ~~what are you doing thing to~~ _____ (do) tonight?

Oh, _____ (leave)?

when are you leaving

Not much. I have to get ready for my trip.

Tomorrow.

Sally and I _____ *are going* (go) out for dinner tonight. Do you want to come?

To the Chinese restaurant across the street.

Well, maybe, Tim. ~~where are you~~ _____ (go)? *going*

[1]

[2]

Did you know? Jack ~~is moving~~ _____ (move) to California.

Hawaii! We'll never see him again.

~~He isn't moving~~ _____ (move) to California. ~~He is moving~~ _____ (move) to Hawaii.

I _____ *I'm having* (have) a party, so I called the Carvers. But they weren't home.

They're away, but ~~they are coming~~ _____ (come) home on Friday.

[3]

[4]

6 ▶ **Talk to your classmates.**

Make a comment to one of your classmates. Your classmate will tell you about a real or imagined future plan. Ask any appropriate questions.

A *You look happy today.*
B *I am. I'm going to a concert tonight.*
A *. . .*

5. What kind of car is that?

Steve's working at the shop when Russell Evans comes in.

1

Russell Hi. I'm having a problem with my car. I heard your ad on the radio and I thought maybe you could fix it.

Steve What's the matter with it?

Russell It's the engine. It's making a funny noise.

Steve Let's take a look at it. Is it parked outside?

Russell Yes. It's over there.

Steve Wow! What kind of car is that?

Russell It's a 1949 Peugeot.

Steve No kidding. Where did you get it?

Russell I bought it from a movie studio in Hollywood.

Steve Really? I've never seen one before. (*He looks under the hood.*)

Russell There aren't too many around. . . . You know, your ad says you can fix anything, but you look a little worried.

Steve Yeah . . . well . . . I'll see what I can do.

(*Thirty minutes later*)

Steve I'm sorry, sir, but I can't find the problem. I've never worked on anything like this before.

Russell But your ad says you can fix anything.

Steve I can. I mean . . . uh . . . it's such an old model. I don't think anyone could fix it.

2. Figure it out

Put the events in the correct order.

4 Steve asked Russell Evans where he got the car.
7 Steve said that he couldn't find the problem.
2 Russell Evans heard Steve's ad on the radio.
5 Russell Evans said that he bought his car from a movie studio in Hollywood.
1 Steve wrote an ad for his shop.
3 Russell Evans brought his car to Steve's shop.
6 Steve tried to fix the car.

📼 3. Listen in

Bob and Margaret are talking about the car that Steve is trying to fix. Read the statements below. Then listen to the conversation and fill in the missing words.

1. The man looks _up set_ .
2. Bob gets _nervous_ when he works on expensive cars.

📼 4. How to say it

Practice the words. Then practice the conversation.

failed	[feyld]	[d]
passed	[pæst]	[t]
wanted	[wantəd]	[əd]

A I think I failed my business test.
B I'm sure you passed.
A I don't know. I wanted to study more, but I was so tired.

5. Your turn

Michael is worried about his business <u>mid-term</u> exam. He's talking to his friend Paul while Bob works on his car. Act out the conversation.

Paul You seem a little depressed. What's the matter?
Michael _I'm worried about my exam._
Paul Why are you worried about it?
Michael _I think I failed_
Paul I'm sure you passed.
Michael _I get nervous when I have to take a test._
Paul A lot of people get nervous.
Michael _I'm stressed (tired)_
Paul You need to take a break. Why don't we go to a movie?
Michael _what movie is playing?_
Paul *The Lost Galaxy* is at the State Theater.
Michael _Good idea._
Paul Great! Let's go.

6.

DEAR MAGGIE

by Margaret Vanderhorn

DEAR MAGGIE: Sometimes I think there's really something wrong with me. I am a college student. I have a few close friends, and I go out on dates <u>occasionally</u>. The <u>trouble</u> starts when I go to a party. I always feel a little nervous before I get there. After I'm there, I get upset with myself because I can't find anything to say to people. I guess I'm just not a <u>good conversationalist</u>. I'm much better when I'm with only a few people. What should I do?
— DEPRESSED

DEAR DEPRESSED: It sounds like you're a little shy. There's nothing wrong with that. Most young people who are shy gain more <u>confidence</u> when they get a little older. In any case, try not to worry about it. If you get upset with yourself, it just makes <u>matters</u> worse. I have a suggestion which could help. Why don't you have a party and invite only your close friends and other people you know well? Small parties can be more fun than big ones. This could also be an opportunity to show how <u>outgoing</u> you really can be.

DEAR MAGGIE: My mother lives in another city, and she comes to visit us for two weeks every year. The problem is that when she comes, she always thinks she has to do everything around the house. My husband and I both work. When we come home in the evening, dinner is ready, the house is <u>absolutely</u> <u>spotless</u>, and the kids have had their baths and are in their pajamas. But my mother has worked so hard that she's nervous, <u>irritable</u>, and very unpleasant to be with for the rest of the evening. I have tried to tell her not to do so much housework, but she won't listen. Is there anything I can do?
— A WORRIED DAUGHTER

DEAR WORRIED DAUGHTER: Your mother probably feels a strong need to be useful, and to prove to you that she's a good guest. But maybe she's also trying to tell you something. It sounds like she's at home most of the day while you and your husband are at work. Maybe she just feels bored and <u>neglected</u> and would like more attention from you. Why don't you schedule her next visit when you can take some time off from work? That way you can share the responsibilities around the house and also get out of the house and do things together. This could make things better.

---

1. **Read the advice column. Then look at each underlined word and choose the best answer.**

1. *Occasionally* means ~~sometimes~~ ~~once in a while~~
   √ a. not very often.
      b. often.

2. *Trouble* means
      a. terrible.
   √ b. problem.

3. A *good conversationalist* is
   √ a. someone who speaks well and talks a lot.
      b. someone who is quiet and doesn't talk much.

4. *Confidence* means
      a. not being sure of one's ability.
   √ b. belief in one's own ability.

5. *Matters* means
   √ a. things.
      b. upset.

6. *Outgoing* means
   √ a. friendly.
      b. unfriendly.

7. *Absolutely* means
   √ a. completely or definitely.
      b. not very.

8. *Spotless* means
      a. very dirty.
   √ b. very clean.

9. *Irritable* means
   √ a. easily made angry by small things.
      b. happy and relaxed.

10. *Neglected* means
      a. getting too much attention.
   ~ b. not getting enough attention.

2. **Do you agree or disagree with the advice Maggie gives to each person?**

PREVIEW

FUNCTIONS/THEMES	LANGUAGE	FORMS
Find out what's wrong	What's the matter? I broke my leg.	
Make a recommendation	I'd better go call for help.	*Had better*
Call for help	My friend just fell off a ladder. Could you send an ambulance?	
Report an emergency	There's a fire at 33 Bank Street.	
Explain what happened	What happened to you? I broke my ankle. When did it happen? The day before yesterday. Did you have to go to the hospital? Yes, I did.	The simple past tense: yes-no questions Expressions of past time
Talk about past activities	Did you have a good weekend? It wasn't bad. What did you do? I went camping.	Review: the simple past tense of irregular verbs

Preview the conversations.

These two women went biking last weekend.
What did you do? Did you have a good time?

Did you ever have an accident? Did you have to get help?
Is there a special telephone number you can call in an emergency?

7. Are you O.K.?

 Anne Burgess and Cindy Wu are on a weekend bike trip.

A

Cindy Anne, watch out!
Anne Wha . . . Oh . . . Ow!
Cindy Are you O.K.?
Anne Uh, I don't think so.
Cindy What's the matter?
Anne I think I broke my ankle. It really hurts.
Cindy I'd better go call for help. Stay here.

backpack   helmet
backsack   strap
back bag
Knapsack
×

B

Operator 911.
Cindy My friend just had a bicycle accident. I think she broke her ankle. Could you send an ambulance?
Operator Could I have your name, please?
Cindy Yes, it's Cindy Wu.
Operator And where's the emergency?
Cindy Near the rest area on Route 60.
Operator All right, Ms. Wu. Stay calm. We'll send an ambulance right away.

C

Nurse What happened?
Anne Oh, I fell off my bike and hurt my ankle. It feels like it's broken.
Nurse Do you have medical insurance, Miss Burgess?
Anne Yes. Would you like to see my insurance card?
Nurse Yes, please. . . . All right. A doctor will be with you in a minute.

D

Pablo Hi, Anne. Did you have a good weekend?

Anne It was so-so.

Pablo What did you do?

Anne Well, I went biking in Evergreen National Park with Cindy Wu, and . . .

Pablo Hey, what happened to you?

Anne That's the bad part. I ran into a rock and fell off my bike. I broke my ankle.

Pablo When did it happen?

Anne The day before yesterday—Saturday. Unfortunately, it was the first day of our trip.

Pablo Did you have to go to the hospital?

Anne Yes, I did. I couldn't walk at all.

Pablo Gee, that's terrible.

Anne Oh, I'll be O.K. in a month or two. So, how was your weekend?

Pablo Not bad. I didn't do anything special. I just stayed home and painted the house.

Figure it out

1. Listen to the conversations and choose the correct answers.

1. a. Cindy had a bicycle accident.
   b. Anne fell off her bike and broke her ankle. ✓
2. a. Anne's ankle will be O.K. in a day or two.
   b. Anne's ankle will be O.K. in a month or two. ✓

2. Listen again and say *True* or *False*.

1. Anne hurt her ankle. T
2. Cindy called 911, the telephone number for emergencies. T
3. An ambulance took Anne to the hospital. T
4. Anne doesn't have medical insurance. F
5. Anne's accident happened the day before yesterday. T
6. Pablo went swimming last weekend. F

3. Match.

1. Are you O.K.?   a. The day before yesterday.
2. What's the matter?   b. I think I broke my ankle.
3. Where's the emergency?   c. Not bad.
4. When did it happen?   d. Near the rest area on Route 60.
5. How was your weekend?   e. I don't think so.

4. Find the simple past tense form of these verbs.

1. fall   fell   3. hurt   hurt   5. have   had
2. break   broke   4. go   went   6. run   ran

8. What's the matter?

toes

1 ► What does each person say? Match the pictures with the sentences.
► Listen to check your answers.

1 crutch
2 crutches
cast

1. b
2. c
3. d
4. e
5. a   *gardening*
6. f   *wheel* *seat* *chain* *pedals* *handlebars*

a. I cut my hand on Saturday, but it wasn't serious. I put on a bandage at home.
b. I broke my leg the day before yesterday. I went to the hospital and they put on a cast.
c. I sprained my ankle yesterday. My friend Bob took me to the doctor, and she put on a bandage.
d. A dog bit me the other day. It didn't hurt very much, but I had to go to the doctor and get a shot.
e. I burned my hand on the stove this morning. My mother put on a bandage.
f. I fell off my bike on my way home from school. It hurts a little, but I'll be all right.

2 ► Listen to the conversation.
► Imagine you had one of the accidents in exercise 1. Act out a similar conversation with a partner.

A What's the matter?
B I broke my leg.
A I'd better go call for help. Stay here.

> **Some recommendations**
>
> I'd better . . .
> go call for help.
> get a doctor.
> put on a bandage.

saw *roof*

3 ► Listen to the conversation. Then check (√) the two things that happened.

___ Jim Garcia fell off the roof.
___ Jim fell off the ladder.
___ There's a fire at 33 Bank Street.
___ Jim burned his hand.
___ Jim had a motorcycle accident.

___ There was a robbery at 33 Bank Street.
___ Jim hurt his back.
___ Jim broke his arm.
___ Jim sprained his wrist.
___ Jim had a heart attack.

above / below the elbow

hammer

4 ► Listen to the conversation.
► Imagine a friend had one of the emergencies in exercise 3. Work with a partner and call for help.

ladder

Operator 911.
Mike My friend just fell off a ladder. Could you send an ambulance?
Operator Could I have your name, please?
Mike Yes, it's Michael Trent.
Operator And where's the emergency?
Mike At 33 Bank Street.
Operator All right, Mr. Trent. Stay calm. We'll send an ambulance right away.

> **Things you might need in an emergency**
>
> Could you send . . .
> a fire truck?
> an ambulance?
> a police car?

5 ► Listen to the two possible conversations.
► Imagine you had one of the accidents in exercise 3. Have a similar conversation with a partner.

A Hey, what happened to you?
B I sprained my ankle.
A When did it happen?
B The day before yesterday.
A Did you have to go to the hospital?

B Yes, I did.   **B** No, I didn't.

Some expressions of past time
yesterday
the day before yesterday
last week/month/year
two weeks/months/years ago

6 ► Study the frame: The simple past tense

Yes-no questions					Short answers		
Did	you he she we they	**have**	to go to the hospital?		Yes,	I he she	**did.**
					No,	we they	**didn't.**

  7 ► Complete the conversations with the correct forms of the simple past tense.
► Listen to check your work.
► Practice the conversations with a partner.

1. John went skiing last weekend and broke his ankle. A friend sees him and thinks he broke his leg. What does the friend ask John?

   Friend Did you break _____ your leg?
   John No, I didn't. I sprained my ~~leg~~ ankle.
                    ~~broke~~

2. The Duponts just moved to California, and they sold their house in New York. Two neighbors are talking about them. What do they say?

   Neighbor 1 Did you hear? The Duponts moved to California.
   Neighbor 2 Really? Did they sell their house?
   Neighbor 1 Yes, they did. A very nice family bought it.

3. Mary usually goes to Thailand on vacation, but this year she went to South Korea. Mary's mother and a friend are talking. What do they say?

   Mother Mary had a wonderful vacation again this year.
   Friend Did she go to Thailand again?
   Mother No, she didn't. She went to South Korea.

4. Betty Smith came back from lunch and found a message. Mr. Jones wants Betty to call him back immediately. What does Betty's secretary ask an hour later?

   Secretary Did you call ~~back~~ Mr. Jones?
   Betty Yes, I did, but no one answered.

8 ► Talk to your classmates. Work in groups. Give a brief description of an emergency you had or saw. Answer your classmates' questions.

9. Did you have a good weekend?

TALK ABOUT PAST ACTIVITIES

  1 ▶ **Listen to these statements. Match each statement with the picture it describes.**

_e_ 1. I went hiking.
_d_ 2. We went biking.
_h_ 3. I went fishing.
_f_ 4. We went camping.
_c_ 5. We went skiing.
_g_ 6. We visited my mother-in-law.
_b_ 7. I didn't go anywhere.
 I stayed home. *and painted the house.*
_a_ 8. I moved into a new apartment.

paint brush

tent
sleeping bag

lantern

picnic basket

pitcher   *chaise longue*
          chaise Lounge

fishing rode
hook
fishing line
fishing reel

---

 2 ▶ **Listen to the conversation.**
▶ **Act out similar conversations with a partner. Use the examples in exercise 1 or your own information.**

A Did you have a good weekend?
B It wasn't bad.
A What did you do?
B I went camping. What did you do?
A I didn't do anything special. I stayed home and worked around the house.

My weekend was . . .	My weekend wasn't . . .
pretty good.	bad.
nice.	great.
relaxing.	too good.
so-so.	much fun.

3 ▶ **Study the frames.**

Review of the simple past tense: Irregular verbs

I	**went** **didn't go**	biking in the mountains.
He	**flew** **didn't fly**	to Paris.
They	**had** **didn't have**	a good time.

Simple past tense of some irregular verbs

bite	**bit**	drive	**drove**	hear	**heard**	run	**ran**
break	**broke**	fall	**fell**	hit	**hit**	say	**said**
bring	**brought**	feel	**felt**	hurt	**hurt**	see	**saw**
buy	**bought**	get	**got**	leave	**left**	sell	**sold**
catch	**caught**	give	**gave**	lose	**lost**	send	**sent**
come	**came**	go	**went**	make	**made**	take	**took**
cut	**cut**	grow	**grew**	meet	**met**	tell	**told**
do	**did**	have	**had**	put	**put**	think	**thought**

See p. 85 for a complete list of irregular verbs.

4 ▶ **Listen to the telephone conversation. Check the travel itinerary the people are talking about.**

Wednesday, July 17   arrive in Paris
Sunday, July 21   fly to Geneva
Monday, July 22   meet Franz
and Helga
Wednesday, July 24   fly home

☐

Wednesday, July 17   arrive in Paris
Saturday, July 20 —
Sunday, July 21   drive to Geneva
Monday, July 22   meet Franz
and Helga
Wednesday, July 24   start trip

☐

5 ▶ **Complete the captions with the simple past tense of the verbs in parentheses.**

1. Franz _____ate_____ the sandwich,
but he _____ate_____ the ant. (eat)
   didn't eat

2. We _____rode_____ all day, but
we _____rode_____ at night. (ride)
   didn't ride

3. Helga _____bought_____ the hat, but she
_____bought_____ the shorts. (buy)
   didn't buy

4. We _____saw_____ Mont Blanc, but we
_____saw_____ the Matterhorn. (see)
   didn't see

6 ▶ **Interview a classmate. Find out if he or she had a good weekend. If it was good, find out what your classmate did. If it wasn't good, find out why.**

10. At least you weren't bored.

Steve drops by Charley's apartment one evening after work.

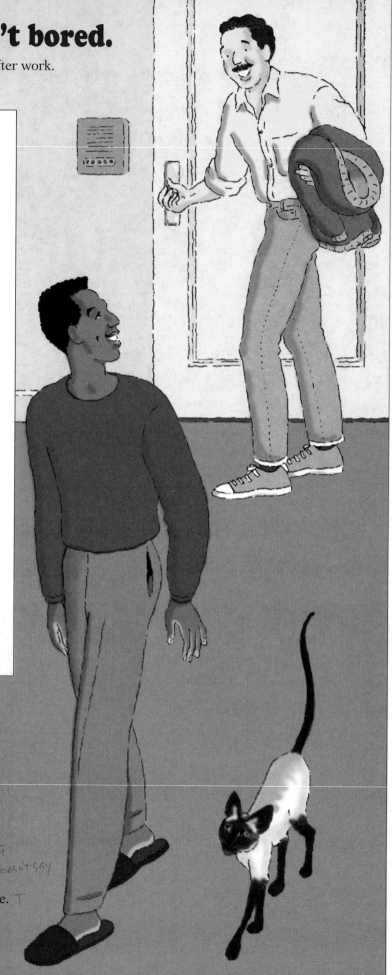

1

Steve Hey, what happened to our best player? We missed you at the game last night. Were you sick or something?

Charley No. I was really tired after work. I tried to call you, but your line was busy. How was the game?

Steve We lost. It wasn't your fault, though. We just didn't play well.

Charley Well, I'll be there next time. By the way, I heard your ad on the radio. It sounds good.

Steve Thanks. But you know, someone heard it and brought in a '49 Peugeot.

Charley A '49 Peugeot? I didn't know that model was still around.

Steve Neither did I. The engine was making a funny noise, and I worked on it for half an hour, but I couldn't fix it.

Charley But your ad says you can fix anything!

Steve I know. The guy with the Peugeot said the same thing. I really felt like an idiot.

Charley It sounds like you had a rough day. But at least you weren't bored. Nothing interesting ever happens at the bank.

Steve No? Are you looking for a new job?

Charley Not yet, but I'm going to start looking soon.

2. Figure it out

Say *True*, *False*, or *It doesn't say*.

1. Charley missed the game because he was sick. F
2. Steve was on the phone with his mother when Charley tried to call. *doesn't say*
3. The team didn't play well, and they lost the game. T
4. Steve can fix anything. F
5. Steve felt like an idiot when he couldn't fix the 1949 Peugeot. T
6. Charley would like a more interesting job. T

3. Your turn

As Steve and Charley are talking, Charley notices Steve's sprained wrist. Act out the conversation.

Charley _What happened ~~with~~ to your hand ~~your arm~~_
Steve I sprained my wrist.
Charley _When did ~~you sprain your wrist~~ it happen?_
Steve Last night, at the soccer game.
Charley _Did you go to the hospital?_
Steve No, I didn't. It wasn't serious enough for the hospital.
Charley _Did ~~you take care of your wrist~~ who took care of it?_
Steve Yeah, my mom took care of it. She's my favorite doctor. By the way, how was your weekend?
Charley _It wasn't bad._
Steve What did you do?
Charley _I didn't do anything special. I stayed home and painted the house_

📼 4. How to say it

Practice the conversation.

A How was your weekend?

B It wasn't bad. I didn't do anything special.

A Did you work?

B No, I didn't.

📼 5. Listen in

While Steve and Charley are talking, a police story is on television. Read the questions below. Then listen to the conversation and choose *a* or *b*.

1. Where's the emergency?
   a. On 18th Street.
   b. On 19th Street. —

2. What's the problem?
   a. Some people are fighting. —
   b. There's a fire.

3. What's the woman's name?
   a. Alice.
   b. She didn't tell the police officer her name. —

Homework

snow cat

11.

RESCUE

*For centuries, people have climbed mountains—
Kilimanjaro in Tanzania, Fuji in Japan, Everest
between Nepal and China. They have climbed
for religious reasons, for reasons of survival, or
just because they were curious. The actual
"sport" of mountain climbing was probably
invented over 200 years ago at Mont Blanc in
the French Alps. Mountain climbing can be a
challenging sport, but it is not without danger
and accidents. The following is an account of a
rescue from Mont Blanc by the brave members
of the Peloton de Gendarmerie de Haute
Montagne (Mountain Rescue Squad), a division
of the French police.*

I had looked forward to this day for a long time. Finally I, Kirsty Stuart, would stand on the top of Mont Blanc, the highest mountain in Europe.

Although I climbed often in my native Scotland, this was my first trip to the Alps. My companions— Jean-Pierre Barton, Maurice Gautier, and Mary Sargent—and I left our camp at the bottom of the mountain early and planned to reach the summit by late morning. The snow was hard and we made good time.

As we neared the top, large clouds gathered and it began to snow. We found shelter and decided to wait for the snow to stop. After three hours, however, we decided to go back and try again the next day. We started down the mountain in the thick snow. Jean-Pierre forgot his sunglasses and went back to look for them. As he was returning to us, he started to fall. "Look out below!" he called.

His fall started an avalanche and it was falling towards us! I was swept away by the heavy snow and landed several meters below. Jean-Pierre hurried down to me. "Are you O.K.?" he asked as he brushed the snow off me.

"I think I broke my leg," I answered.

"I'd better radio for help!" he said. "Where are the others?" We couldn't see Maurice or Mary anywhere.

Jean-Pierre called the emergency radio number, and the police said they would send help right away. It seemed like hours, but only minutes later we heard the welcome sound of a helicopter. Jean-Pierre waved his bright orange jacket in the air. The helicopter couldn't land on the mountainside, so they lowered two men, two dogs, and a stretcher. One man ran to me, but I told him to search for the others. The dogs were trained for avalanche rescue and soon began to dig frantically in the snow. "They've found them!" Jean-Pierre called.

Bernardo, the lead dog, found Mary's scarf and led the rescuers to her. Maurice was nearby. The men gave us hot drinks and warm blankets and then prepared to lift us into the helicopter. Two men inside the helicopter pulled us up by the ropes. I went first on the stretcher.

Once we were safely inside, the helicopter flew to the hospital in Chamonix. Our poor rescuers and their dogs had to climb all the way back down the mountain. Later we would find these brave men and thank them for saving our lives.

*sweep
swept swept*

1. Read the magazine article. Then scan the article and find:

a. how many climbers there were.   *four*
b. the name of the mountain they tried to climb.   *Mont Blanc*
c. how many rescuers there were.   *two rescuer*
d. the location of the hospital.   *in Chamonix*

2. Discuss these questions.

1. How did the avalanche start?
2. Who found Mary Sargent?   *Bernardo , the lead dog*
3. Would you like to go mountain climbing? Why or why not?

FUNCTIONS/THEMES	LANGUAGE	FORMS
Get to know someone	Where are you from originally? I'm from Argentina. How long have you lived in New York? I've been here for five years. I've been here since 1990.	The present perfect: information questions and statements *For* and *since*
Keep a conversation going Talk about abilities	So, you're from Argentina. Uh-huh. I'd like to go to South America someday. Do you know how to speak Spanish? A little. Where did you learn it? I studied it in school.	*Know how to*
Give someone a message	Did anyone call? Yes. Someone named Sharon Kennedy. What did she want? She wants you to call her back at work.	Object pronouns: *me, you, him, her, us, them* Direct and indirect objects
Instruct someone politely	Someone ordered these sandwiches. Could you give them to the woman over there? Sure.	*Could*
Get the correct change	Excuse me. I think I gave you a twenty. Oh, then I owe you ten dollars. I'm very sorry.	

Preview the conversations.

These two people don't know each other. However, they feel free to talk to each other because they have something in common: they like the same music. Is it acceptable in your country to strike up a conversation with a stranger when you notice that you both have things in common?

12. I really need a break.

 Luis is a cashier at Endicott Booksellers in New York City. He is having a busy day.

A

Luis Hello. Endicott Booksellers.
Sharon I'd like to speak to Marcia, please.
Luis Marcia's at lunch. Can I take a message?
Sharon Yes. Please tell her that Sharon Kennedy called, and ask her to call me back at work. She has the number.
Luis O.K. I'll give her the message.

B

Delivery man Hi. I'm from Ralph's Coffee Shop. Somebody ordered these sandwiches.
Luis Oh, right. Could you give them to the woman over there? She ordered them.
Delivery man Sure.

C

Luis José Luis Rodríguez—El Puma. You chose a good CD.
Customer Do you think so?
Luis Yes. He wrote all the lyrics and they're really beautiful.
Customer Oh, can you speak Spanish?
Luis Yes, I speak it fluently. It was my first language.
Customer Where are you from originally?
Luis Well, I was born in Venezuela.
Customer Really? How long have you lived in New York?
Luis Oh, I grew up here. I've been in New York since I was ten.
Customer I'd like to go to South America someday.
Luis Would you?
Customer Yeah. I imagine it's very interesting.
Luis Do you know how to speak Spanish?
Customer Not very well, but I'm learning. I speak Portuguese, though.
Luis Oh? Where did you learn Portuguese?
Customer I studied it in college.
Luis Well, then maybe Spanish will be easy for you.
Customer I hope so, but they're very different languages.
Luis So, that's $8.95 . . . and here's your change.
Customer Excuse me. I think I gave you a twenty.
Luis Oh, then I <u>owe</u> you ten dollars. I'm very sorry.
Customer No problem.

Marcia Hi, Luis. I'm back. Did anyone call?
Luis Yes. Someone named Sharon Kennedy.
Marcia What did she want?
Luis She wants you to call her back at work.
Marcia Anyone else?
Luis No, that's all.
Marcia O.K. Did you have lunch?
Luis No, I didn't have time. I was too busy.
Marcia Why don't you go out now? I'll <u>take over</u> for you.
Luis Thanks a lot. I really need a break.

Figure it out

l. Listen to the conversations and choose *a, b,* or *c.*

1. a. Luis speaks Spanish.
   b. The customer speaks Spanish.
   c. Both Luis and the customer speak Spanish.

2. a. First, Luis gives the customer the right change.
   b. First, Luis gives the customer the wrong change.
   c. First, Luis gives the customer no change.

2. Listen again. Say *True, False,* or *It doesn't say.*

1. The sandwiches from the coffee shop are for Luis. F
2. Endicott Booksellers sells books and CDs only in English. It doesn't say
3. Luis was born in South America. T
4. Luis has lived in New York since he was 10 years old. T
5. The customer often travels to South America. F
6. Luis took a telephone message for Marcia. T
7. Marcia doesn't have time to call Sharon back. It doesn't say
8. Luis is tired. T

3. Find another way to say it.

1. That's O.K.   *No problem.*
2. Can you speak Spanish?   Do you know to speak —?
3. You should go out now.   Why don't you go out now?
4. I'll take your place.   I'll take over for you.
5. I need a rest.   I need a break

13. Where are you from originally?

  1 ▶ **Listen to the conversation and complete the information about each person.**

1. _____ is from Kenya originally. He has lived in New York for _____ years.

2. _____ grew up in Washington. She has lived in New York since _____ .

3. _____ is originally from Japan. She has lived in New York since _____ .

4. _____ is from Argentina originally. He has lived in New York for _____ years.

Abdul

Magumi

Aldo

Dee

  2 ▶ **Listen to the conversation.**
▶ **Practice the conversation with a partner. Use your own information.**

A Where are you from originally?
B I'm from Argentina.
A How long have you lived in New York?
B I've been here for five years.

> Use *for* with a period of time.
> Use *since* with a specific time or date.
>
> I've been here . . .
> | | |
> |---|---|
> | for two months. | since 1990. |
> | for five years. | since October. |
> | for a long time. | since I was 10. |

3 ▶ **Study the frames: The present perfect**

Information questions				
How long	**have**	you we they	**lived** **been**	in New York?
	has	he she		

Affirmative and negative statements			
I We You They	**have ('ve)** **haven't**	**lived** **been**	here for ten years. here very long.
He She	**has ('s)** **hasn't**	**lived** **been**	here since October. here very long.

Base form	Simple past	Past participle
be	was, were	**been***
live	lived	**lived**
work	worked	**worked**

*See p. 85 for the past participles of irregular verbs.

4 ▶ **Complete this article from an employee newsletter. Use the present perfect of the verbs in parentheses.**

This week our spotlight is on Magumi Saito, the new manager of our Far East department. Ms. Saito is originally from Kyoto. She _____ (not be) in New York very long. In fact, she _____ (be) here for only two months, but she _____ (live) in the United States since 1990, when she attended Boston University. She _____ (work) for Danton Bookstores for one year, first in Boston and now in New York. Ms. Saito holds a master's degree in international business and says she _____ (be) interested in the book business for a long time. She is also a collector of old books. And how long _____ she _____ (collect) books? "I _____ (collect) books since I was a child," Ms. Saito reports.

5 ▶ Listen to two ways to continue the conversation in exercise 2.
▶ Act out a similar conversation with a partner.

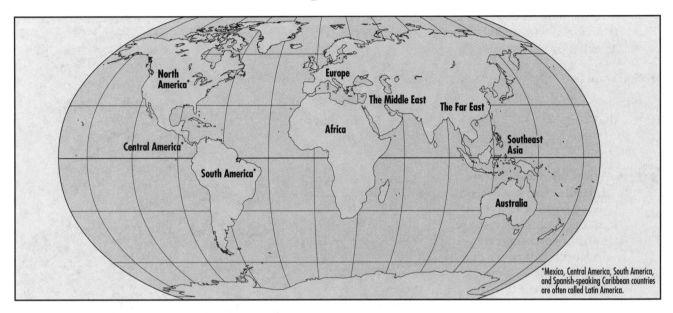

Mexico, Central America, South America, and Spanish-speaking Caribbean countries are often called Latin America.

A So, you're from Argentina.
B Uh-huh.

A I'd like to go to South America someday.	**A** I've been to Argentina.
B Would you?	**B** Really? How did you like it?
A Yeah. I imagine it's very interesting.	**A** It was very interesting.
B Do you know how to speak Spanish?	**B** Do you know how to speak Spanish?
A A little.	**A** No, I don't. Unfortunately, I'm not very good at languages.
B Where did you learn it?	
A I studied it in school.	

> **Do you know how to speak . . .?**
>
> Yes, I speak it fluently.
> We spoke it at home.
> A little.
> I studied it in school.
> Not very well.
> A friend taught me.
> No, I don't.
> I'm not very good at languages.

 6 ▶ Listen to the continuation of the conversation from exercise 5.
Check (√) the things Aldo and Magumi like and know how to do.

Languages	English	Spanish	Japanese	Music	Spanish music	American music	Japanese music	Musical Instruments	The piano	The guitar	The violin	Sports	Play tennis	Swim	Ski
Aldo knows how to speak				Aldo likes				Aldo can play				Aldo knows how to			
Magumi knows how to speak				Magumi likes				Magumi can play				Magumi knows how to			

7 ▶ Find out where a classmate is from originally, and find out how long he or she has been in this city. Use your imagination and keep the conversation going.

14. Did anyone call?

1
- ▶ **Listen to the two possible conversations.**
- ▶ **Practice the conversations with a partner.**

A Hi, I'm back. Did anyone call?
B Yes. Someone named Sharon Kennedy.
A What did she want?

B She wants you to call her back at work.
A Anyone else?
B No, that's all.

B She didn't leave a message.
A Anyone else?
B No, that's all.

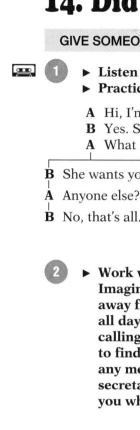

For _Marcia Hines_
Date _4/25_   Time _1:00_
WHILE YOU WERE OUT
M _s. Sharon Kennedy_
From _____
Phone No. _____
☑ TELEPHONED   ☐ URGENT
☐ PLEASE CALL   ☐ WANTS TO SEE YOU
☐ WILL CALL AGAIN   ☐ CAME TO SEE YOU
☐ RETURNED YOUR CALL
Message _She wants you to call her back at work._ _LG_

2
- ▶ **Work with a partner. Imagine you have been away from your office all day and now you are calling your secretary to find out if there are any messages. Your secretary will tell you who called.**

For _(Your name)_
Date _4/25_   Time _2:00_
WHILE YOU WERE OUT
M _r. Bill Raines_
From _London_
Phone No. _____
☑ TELEPHONED   ☐ URGENT
☐ PLEASE CALL   ☐ WANTS TO SEE YOU
☐ WILL CALL AGAIN   ☐ CAME TO SEE YOU
☐ RETURNED YOUR CALL
Message _He's really sorry, but he can't meet you for dinner. He lost his passport and is still in England._

For _(Your name)_
Date _4/25_   Time _3:15_
WHILE YOU WERE OUT
M _s. Rita Parsons_
From _____
Phone No. _555-2101_
☑ TELEPHONED   ☐ URGENT
☐ PLEASE CALL   ☐ WANTS TO SEE YOU
☐ WILL CALL AGAIN   ☐ CAME TO SEE YOU
☐ RETURNED YOUR CALL
Message _She's in town until Sunday. She's staying at her brother's, and you can reach her there after 6:00._

For _(Your name)_
Date _4/25_   Time _4:30_
WHILE YOU WERE OUT
M _s. Karen Chiang_
From _Personnel department_
Phone No. _x 2619_
☑ TELEPHONED   ☐ URGENT
☐ PLEASE CALL   ☐ WANTS TO SEE YOU
☐ WILL CALL AGAIN   ☐ CAME TO SEE YOU
☐ RETURNED YOUR CALL
Message _____

3
- ▶ **Study the frames.**

Object pronouns

	indirect object			direct object
He gave	**me** **you** **him** **her** **us** **them**	the message	when he saw	**me.** **you.** **him.** **her.** **us.** **them.**

Direct and indirect objects

	indirect object	direct object
He gave	Marcia her	the message.

	direct object		indirect object
He gave	the message it	to	Marcia. her.

When the direct object is a pronoun, *to* + the indirect object follows.

4
- ▶ **Jim and Alice work together. Complete their conversations, using direct and indirect objects.**
- ▶ **Listen to check your work.**
- ▶ **Practice the conversations with a partner.**

1. **Man** Can I speak to Jim, please?
   Alice He isn't here right now. Can I *give him a message*?
   Man Yes. Could you tell him Jack called?
   Alice Sure.

2. **Jim** Alice, could you give this book to Mr. Wilson?
   Alice I already did. _I gave it to him_ last week.
   Jim Oh, thanks. You remember everything.

3. **Alice** There's a message from Stan and Marcy Miller. Do you know them? _they bought my house._
   Jim Of course. (_I know them._) _I sold my house to them. them my house._
   Alice The Millers bought your old house? I didn't know that.

4. **Alice** Oh, look. Your friend Jack left his gloves here.
   Jim No problem. We're going to the gym together later, so I'll _give them_ . _to him. him the gloves_

15. I think I gave you a twenty.

INSTRUCT SOMEONE POLITELY • *COULD*

1 ▶ Complete the conversations with polite instructions. Use the instructions in the box.
▶ Listen to check your work.
▶ Practice the conversations with a partner.

> Take it to the Lost and Found.
> Put it in an envelope and save it.
> Give them to him tomorrow.
> Give them to the woman over there.

1. **A** Someone ordered these sandwiches.
   B *Could you give them to the woman over there?*
   A Sure.

2. **A** Someone left some change by the cash register.
   B Could you put it in an envelope and save it?
   A O.K. I'm sure someone will come back for it.

3. **A** Someone left a wallet here.
   B Could you take it to the Lost and found?
   A O.K.

4. **A** Your assistant went home and forgot these.
   B Could you give them to him tomorrow?
   A All right. I'll put them in my desk.

GET THE CORRECT CHANGE

2 ▶ Listen to the conversation between a cashier and a customer. Then choose *a* or *b*.

1. The customer bought
   a. a book.
   b. some photographs.

2. The customer wants the cashier
   a. to put them in a bag.
   b. to put it in a box.

3. The customer
   a. paid cash for his purchase.
   b. charged his purchase.

4. The customer gave the cashier
   a. a twenty-dollar bill.
   b. a fifty-dollar bill.

3 ▶ Listen to the conversation.
▶ Act out a similar conversation with a partner. Use the information in the table.

Cashier So, that's $8.95. And here's your change.
Customer Excuse me. I think I gave you a twenty.
Cashier Oh, then I owe you ten dollars. I'm very sorry.
Customer No problem.

The price is:	You gave the cashier:	The cashier gave you:
$ 8.95	$20.00	$1.05
$ 6.95	$20.00	$3.05
$ 3.69	$10.00	$1.31
$19.95	$50.00	$ .05

16. Do you speak Hungarian?

Emma Kovacs and Tom Anderson are at the Hollywood Bowl, a large outdoor theater in Los Angeles. They're going to see an Italian opera.

1

Tom It certainly is beautiful here.

Emma It really is. Oh, look. Peter Kadar is singing tonight.

Tom I don't think I've ever heard of him.

Emma He's a well-known Hungarian singer, and he performs in the U.S. every year. I'm always interested in Hungarian performers. My parents were both musicians from Hungary.

Tom Oh, is Kovacs a Hungarian name?

Emma Well, Kovacs is my married name. But, yes, my husband was Hungarian, too.

Tom That's interesting. Do you speak Hungarian?

Emma Yes, we spoke it at home when I was a child. I also spoke it with my husband from time to time.

Tom My parents came here from Sweden, so I speak a little Swedish, but I didn't marry a Swedish woman. In fact, I've never been married.

Emma Well, airline pilots travel a lot, so I suppose it's hard to have a family.

Tom Not really. Most airline pilots get married. I just never wanted to settle down.

Emma I can understand that. I got married right after I finished medical school, and I never had a free moment after that.

Tom A doctor's life must be very hard.

Emma Well, sometimes it is. . . . Look, here comes the conductor.

2. Figure it out

Say *True*, *False*, or *It doesn't say*.

1. One of the opera singers is Hungarian.
2. Emma learned to speak Hungarian from her parents.
3. Emma's husband spoke Hungarian.
4. Emma's children speak Hungarian.
5. Tom speaks Swedish fluently.
6. Tom didn't get married because he didn't have time for a family.
7. Emma got married before she went to medical school.

📼 3. Listen in

Look at the people in the audience below. Then listen to the conversations and match each conversation with the appropriate people.

Conversation 1	a
Conversation 2	b
Conversation 3	c

📼 4. How to say it

Practice the phrase below. Then practice the conversation.

did you   [dɪdʒu]

A Where did you learn Japanese?
B I lived in Japan for two years.
A Did you study it before you went there?
B Yes. I studied it in college.

5. Your turn

Two musicians, Andrea Lanza and Mark Crespi, are talking to each other before the opera begins. Mark is a new member of the orchestra. Take the role of Andrea or Mark and act out the conversation. Use this information.

Andrea was born in Brazil but grew up in Miami. She spoke English at home with her parents.	Mark's from Los Angeles, but his parents are from Italy. He spoke Italian at home with them.
Andrea asks if Mark understands Italian.	Mark says he speaks it fluently.
She asks where he learned Italian.	He says where he learned Italian.
She says she'd like to go to Italy someday.	He asks where Andrea is from.
She says where she's from.	He asks if she speaks Portuguese.
She tells why she forgot all her Portuguese.	

17.

Kiri Te Kanawa

by Sylvia P. Bloch

The international opera world knows Kiri Te Kanawa for her beautiful appearance and excellent soprano voice. In her late forties, she has appeared in the film version of the opera Don Giovanni, *and millions saw her on television when she sang at the wedding of the Prince and Princess of Wales. In 1982, she was made a Dame of the British Empire.*

Interviewer: Dame Te Kanawa, could you tell me a little about your background?

Te Kanawa: I was born in New Zealand, in the town of Gisborne. My father was Maori, a native Polynesian, and my mother's family was Irish.

Interviewer: Are there any other musicians in your family?

Te Kanawa: Well, my mother played the piano for pleasure—I think she really wanted to be a performer. When I was three, she decided that I would be a singer, and when I was seven, I started playing the piano.

Interviewer: I know opera singers train for many years. Did you grow up and receive your training in New Zealand?

Te Kanawa: Partly. When I was eleven, my family moved to Auckland—that's the largest city in New Zealand—so I could have singing lessons. Then when I was eighteen, my mother and I left New Zealand and moved to London, where I studied at the London Opera Centre.

Interviewer: What are your other interests—besides the opera?

Te Kanawa: I enjoy swimming, playing golf, and sewing, but most of all I enjoy spending time with my family.

Interviewer: Tell me about your family.

Te Kanawa: I'm married and have two children, a son and a daughter. We make our home in Surrey, near London.

Interviewer: How do you manage to balance your home life with your singing career?

Te Kanawa: I perform in opera houses all over the world, but I try not to take jobs that keep me away from my family for a long time. The summers are especially important, and we take the children to Portugal. My music, my family, and my friends are very important to me. I do everything I can to have time for all of them.

1. Read the interview and answer the questions.

1. What does Dame Kiri Te Kanawa do for a living?
2. Where is she from originally?
3. How long has she lived in England?
4. What are her interests besides the opera?

2. The interview above is not a real interview. The author only imagined talking to Kiri Te Kanawa. Imagine you are planning to interview a famous person. Who will you interview, and what questions will you ask?

FUNCTIONS/THEMES	LANGUAGE	FORMS
Talk about plans	Will you be around this summer? Yes, I will. I've got a job at the YMCA. Maybe I'll take summer classes. I'll probably take summer classes.	The future with *will*: information questions; statements; yes-no questions and short answers *Maybe* and *probably*
Wish someone well	Have a good summer. Thanks. You too. And good luck on your interview. Thanks. I'll need it.	
Ask for and give directions	Excuse me. How far is the National Theater from here? About three blocks. How do I get there? Walk down F Street to Fourteenth Street and turn right. Is this the way to the personnel office? Yes, it is. Go down the hall and to the right.	
Thank someone	Thank you very much. My pleasure.	
Interview for a job	I'm looking for a summer job. Are you interested in working full time? Yes, I am.	Preposition + gerund
Talk about school	Where do you go to school? I go to George Washington University. When will you graduate? Next June.	
Talk about skills and interests	Do you have any special skills or interests? Well, I can use a computer and I know how to speak Spanish. And in my free time, I like to read.	

Preview the conversations.

American colleges and universities often have students from other cities, states, and countries. During the long summer vacation, most of these students go home, but some stay and get jobs. How do students in your country spend their school vacations?

18. Interview

 Meg Harper and Jim Cruz are students at George Washington University in Washington, D.C. Today is the last day before summer vacation.

A

Meg Will you be around this summer, Jim?
Jim No, I won't. I'm going to spend the summer at home with my parents.
Meg Where's that?
Jim New Orleans. What are you going to do?
Meg I'm not sure yet. I've got an interview at the *Washington Post* at one today, so maybe I'll get a job there.
Jim Oh, yeah? That sounds interesting.
Meg Yeah. I'm keeping my fingers crossed.
Jim Well, I probably won't see you before I leave, so have a good summer.
Meg Thanks. You too.
Jim And good luck on your interview.
Meg Thanks. I'll need it.

B

Meg Excuse me. How far is Fifteenth Street from here? I'm looking for the *Washington Post*.
Man About two blocks. It's between Vermont Avenue and Sixteenth Street.
Meg Thanks a lot.
Man My pleasure.

C

Meg Excuse me. Is this the way to the personnel department?
Woman Yes, it is. Go down the hall and to the right. It's across from the cafeteria.
Meg Thank you.

D

Mr. Reed So, you're looking for a summer job. Are you interested in working full time?

Meg Yes, I am.

Mr. Reed And where do you go to school?

Meg George Washington University.

Mr. Reed Oh, yes. I see that on your application. When will you graduate?

Meg Next June. I only have one more year.

Mr. Reed Do you have any special <u>skills</u> or interests?

Meg Well, I can use a computer and I know how to speak Spanish. And in my free time, I like to read.

E

Meg Thank you very much, Mr. Reed. I'm really excited about the job.

Mr. Reed Well, I think you'll enjoy working for the *Post*.

Figure it out

1. Listen to the conversations. Then choose *a* or *b*.

1. This summer Jim is going to
   a. stay in Washington, D.C.
   b. go home.

2. This summer Meg is going to
   a. work at the *Washington Post*.
   b. take classes at George Washington University.

2. Listen again and say *True, False,* or *It doesn't say*.

1. Jim's parents live in Washington, D.C. T
2. Jim is going to work this summer. F
3. The *Washington Post* is on Fifteenth Street. T
4. The personnel department is on the second floor. *It doesn't say*
5. Meg wants to work all year. F
6. Meg is going to be a reporter at the *Washington Post*. *doesn't say*

3. Match.

1. Will you be around this summer?
2. What are you going to do?
3. Good luck on your interview.
4. How far is Fifteenth Street from here?
5. Where do you go to school?
6. When will you graduate?

a. No, I won't.
b. About two blocks.
c. Next June.
d. George Washington University.
e. Thanks. I'll need it.
f. I'm not sure yet.

19. Will you be around this summer?

 1 ► Sam, Pam, Andy, Sue, and Bob are university students. What are they going to do during their summer vacation? Listen and then complete the sentences with the name of the correct person.

1. ___Sam___ is going home for the summer.

2. ___Pam___ is going to work in a law office.

3. _____ is taking summer classes. Andy

4. ___Bob___ has got a job as a lifeguard.

5. _____ doesn't know what she's going to do. Sue

  2 ► Listen to the two possible conversations.
► Act out a similar conversation with a partner. Use your own information.

A Will you be around this summer?

B Yes, I will. I've got a job at the YMCA. What are you going to do?

A I'm not sure yet. Maybe I'll stay and take summer classes.

B No, I won't. I'm going to spend the summer at home with my parents. What are you going to do?

A I'm not sure yet. I've got an interview today, so maybe I'll get a job.

Will you be around . . .

this summer?
over the vacation?
over the holidays?
during the semester break?

Maybe and *probably* are often used with *will.*

Maybe I'll take summer classes. (not sure yet)
I'll probably take summer classes. (almost sure)

3 ▶ **Listen to the rest of the second conversation in exercise 2.**
▶ **Imagine you are leaving for vacation. Wish your partner well.**

B Well, I probably won't see you before I leave, so have a good summer.
A Thanks. You too.
B And good luck on your interview.
A Thanks. I'll need it.

Have a good . . .	And good luck on your . . .
summer.	interview.
vacation.	test.
trip.	job.

4 ▶ **Study the frames: The future with *will***

Information questions					Affirmative and negative statements		
When	will	you she it we they	be there?		I She It We They	**will** (**'ll**)	**be** there tomorrow.
						will not (**won't**)	**be** there until late.

Yes-no questions	Short answers
Will you **be** here tomorrow?	Yes, I **will**. No, I **won't**.

 5 ▶ **Complete the conversation with *will* and the verbs in parentheses.**
▶ **Listen to check your work.**
▶ **Practice the conversation with a partner.**

A I think I _will go_ (go) to Boston during the break. Why don't you come along? (with me)
B Oh, I don't know. Where _will we stay_ (stay)?
A We _will find_ (find) a cheap hotel somewhere.
B I _will have to_ (have to) think about it. When do you need to know?
A Sometime this weekend.
B O.K. I _will call_ (call) you.
A I _will not be_ →won't (not be) home tomorrow during the day, but I _will be_ (be) here tomorrow night.
B _Will you be_ (be) home on Sunday?
A Yes.
B Good. I _will call_ (call) you then. I have three final exams next week, so I _will be_ (be) at the library all day tomorrow and I probably _will not get_ (not get) home won't until late.
A O.K. I _will talk_ (talk) to you Sunday.
B Fine.

6 ▶ **Interview a classmate. Find out what he or she is going to do this summer or during the next school break. Tell your classmate what you are going to do.**

Unit 4 **37**

20. How far is Fifteenth Street from here?

1 ▶ Listen to the conversation.
▶ Act out a similar conversation with a partner.

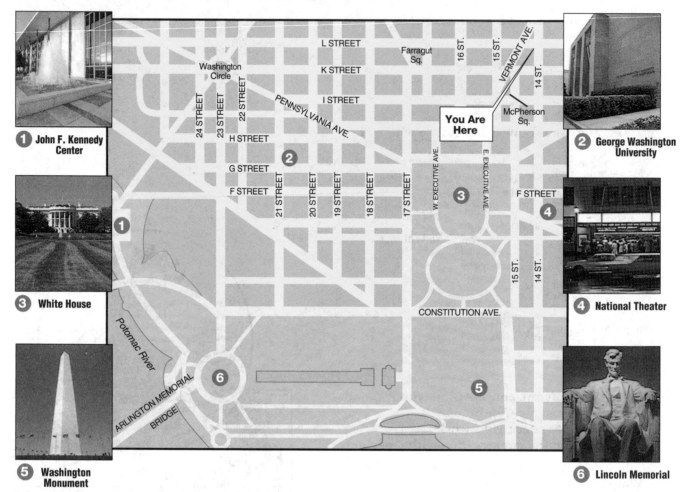

1 John F. Kennedy Center

2 George Washington University

3 White House

4 National Theater

5 Washington Monument

6 Lincoln Memorial

A Excuse me. How far is Fifteenth Street from here?
B About two blocks. (It's between Vermont Avenue and Sixteenth Street.)
A Thank you very much.
B My pleasure.

2 ▶ Where is the man going? Listen to the directions and find the place on the map above.

3 ▶ Listen to the conversation.
▶ Imagine you are at the White House in Washington, D.C. Act out a similar conversation and ask for directions to one of the other places on the map.

A Excuse me. How far is the National Theater from here?
B Oh, about three blocks.
A How do I get there?
B Walk down F Street to Fourteenth Street and turn right. Go straight ahead about a block, and it should be on your left.

medical supplies

21. Are you interested in working full time?

ASK FOR AND GIVE DIRECTIONS • INTERVIEW FOR A JOB • TALK ABOUT SCHOOL • TALK ABOUT SKILLS AND INTERESTS

 1 ▶ **Listen to the conversation.**
▶ **Imagine you are looking for one of the places at the *Washington Post*. Act out a similar conversation with a partner.**

A Excuse me. Is this the way to the personnel department?
B Yes, it is. Go down the hall and to the right. It's across from the cafeteria.
A Thank you.

where did you go to School
study

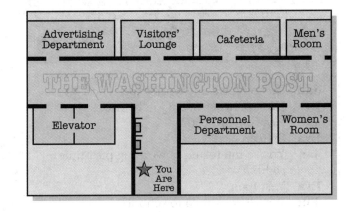

  2 ▶ **Listen to the two conversations.**
▶ **Practice the conversations with a partner.**

A I'm looking for a summer job.
B Are you interested in working full time?
A Yes, I am.
B And where do you go to school?
A I go to George Washington University.
B When will you graduate?
A Next June.
B Do you have any special skills or interests?
A Well, I can use a computer and I know how to speak Spanish. And in my free time, I like to read.

A I'm looking for a summer job.
B Are you interested in working full time?
A No, I'd like to work part time.
B And where do you go to school?
A I went to George Washington University.
B When did you graduate?
A In 1992.
B Do you have any special skills or interests?
A Well, I can use a computer and I know how to speak Spanish. And in my free time, I like to read.

Preposition + gerund

be interested **in** working

  3 ▶ **Another applicant is interviewing for a job. Listen to the interview and check (√) the appropriate items on the interviewer's checklist.**

4 ▶ **Play these roles.**

Student A You are the director of personnel for a small company. Use the Interviewer's Checklist above and interview Student B.

Student B You are in the personnel office of a small company and are applying for a job. Answer Student A's questions.

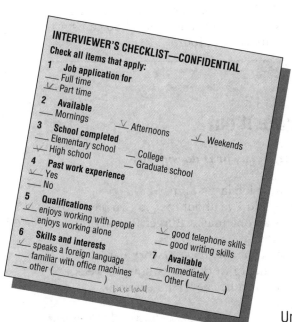

INTERVIEWER'S CHECKLIST—CONFIDENTIAL
Check all items that apply:
1 Job application for
— Full time
√ Part time
2 Available
— Mornings   √ Afternoons   √ Weekends
3 School completed
— Elementary school
√ High school   — College   — Graduate school
4 Past work experience
√ Yes
— No
5 Qualifications
√ enjoys working with people
— enjoys working alone   √ good telephone skills   — good writing skills
6 Skills and interests
√ speaks a foreign language
— familiar with office machines   7 Available
— other (_____)   — Immediately   — Other (_____)
baseball

22. How soon can you start?

Bonnie Perkins called Eva and told her there was an opening at Burger Ranch. Eva has an interview with Jan Souza, the manager of Burger Ranch.

Burger Ranch

Hamburger		$2.39
Cheeseburger		2.69
Chicken sandwich		3.19
Fish sandwich		3.49
Ranch salad		2.29
French fries	lg.	1.19
	sm.	.79
DRINKS		
Coffee/Tea		.89
Milk		1.09
Soda	lg.	1.39
	sm.	.89
Milkshake		1.49
DESSERTS		
Ranch chocolate chip cookie		.89
Apple pie		1.39

1

Jan Do you have any work experience, Eva?
Eva No, I've never had a job before.
Jan How old are you?
Eva Sixteen.
Jan You're interested in working part time, right?
Eva Yes, I am.
Jan Where do you go to school?
Eva I'm a junior at Susan B. Anthony High School.
Jan Oh, that's right. You and Bonnie go to the same school. Well, about the job—it gets very busy here in the evenings. You have to work fast, and there's a lot of pressure.
Eva That's no problem.
Jan I'm looking for someone dependable. Will you be here every afternoon at four?
Eva Oh, yes. I'm always on time.
Jan The hours are four to eight, Monday through Friday. You'll make five dollars an hour. How does that sound?
Eva That sounds fine.
Jan Oh, and you'll get a free meal every evening. Do you like hamburgers?
Eva I love them.
Jan Well, I think you'll like it here. How soon can you start?
Eva Can I start today?
Jan Today?
Eva Yeah. I mean, there's no rush. I'm just anxious to start.
Jan Well, first you have to get a uniform and some comfortable shoes. You can start tomorrow at four.

2. Figure it out

Say *True, False,* or *It doesn't say.*

1. Eva had a job last summer.
2. Bonnie told Eva about the job two days ago.
3. There's an opening at Burger Ranch on weekends.
4. Eva will probably have to work hard.
5. Eva's going to work twenty hours a week.
6. Eva will start her new job next week.

40 Unit 4

(handwritten: visual dictionary "chapters")

🔊 3. Listen in

The man below is asking for directions. Read the questions. Then listen to the conversation and answer the questions.

1. What street is Pacific Electronics on? *(handwritten: 60 street)*
2. How far is Pacific Electronics from Burger Ranch? *(handwritten: 2 miles)*

🔊 4. How to say it

Practice the words below. Then practice the conversation.

I'll	
you'll	**A** I'll be here tomorrow.
he'll	**B** What about Jim?
we'll	**A** He'll come around ten.
they'll	**B** And Bob and Sherry?
	A They'll be here, too.
	B Oh, then we'll all be here.
	A You mean you'll be here, too?
	B Of course.

(handwritten labels: baseball bat, baseball cap, singlet, camisole, sleeveless T-shirt, short-sleeved T-shirt, long-sleeved T-shirt, collar, sleeve, cuff, tail)

5. Your turn

Eva runs into her friend Rick on her way home from Burger Ranch. She tells him about her new job. Act out the conversation.

Rick Hi, Eva. *(handwritten: How are you doing?)*
Eva *(handwritten: Hi Rick, How are you?)*
Rick Fine. Listen, will you be around tomorrow after school?
Eva *(handwritten: No I won't. I just got a new job.)* *(found)*
Rick That's great! What are your hours?
Eva *(handwritten: from 4 to 8 Monday to Friday.)*
Rick Is the pay good?
Eva *(handwritten: It's 5 dollars an hour.)*
Rick Well, I have to go now. Good luck on your new job.
Eva *(handwritten: Thanks...)*

Unit 4 **41**

23.

WHERE WILL WE GO FROM HERE?

high definition

In the twentieth century, many inventions brought quick and dramatic change to our lives. Consider, for example, the electric light. During the 1870s, two inventors, Joseph Swan in England and Thomas Edison in the United States, perfected their models of electric lamps. By December 1882, 203 customers in New York City were living and working by the light of 3,144 electric lamps. The distribution of electricity to the public led the way to many conveniences we take for granted in our homes today: the radio, the automatic washing machine, the air conditioner, and many others.

In 1903, the Wright brothers built and flew the first airplane with a motor. Their first flight lasted only 12 seconds and went only 120 feet (about 36 meters). By 1970, the Boeing 747 jumbo jet carried 350 people across the Atlantic Ocean from the United States to Europe in about 7 hours. In 1976, service started on the Concorde, a plane developed by the French and British that travels faster than the speed of sound. However, probably nothing about air travel can compare to an event in 1969: approximately 60 years after the first flight of an airplane, astronauts landed on the moon!

In addition to wanting to travel and learn more about the world, people wanted better and quicker communication with each other. The first telephone conversation was in 1876, when an American, Alexander Graham Bell, spoke on his invention to an assistant in another room. Today, telephones are everywhere —even in cars. We can speak to a single person or to many people at once. Soon we will be able to see the person we are talking to on video-telephones (some models are available now). We can already send pictures by phone using a fax machine, and we can even hook up computers to telephones in order to transfer information back and forth.

It took many years and many people to develop television technology, but by the 1950s, everyone was interested in owning a television set. In the 1960s, satellites made it possible for people to watch events happening across the globe. Since the 1970s, TVs have gotten bigger—and smaller. VCRs make it possible to record TV shows and watch them later, and video cameras give people the chance to make their own movies to watch. People even play video games on their TVs. It is amazing to realize that in less than 50 years from the early experiments with television, the "Live Aid" concert on TV in 1985 was watched by 1.5 billion people around the world.

1,500,000,000 (one point five billion)

About a hundred years ago the electric light, the telephone, the TV, and the airplane did not exist. These scientific developments have changed our lives in a very short time. As we enter the twenty-first century, we might wonder "Where will we go from here?"

1. **Look at the title of the magazine article and the pictures. What do you think the article is about?**

2. **Read the article. Then scan it and find at least ten things that did not exist about a century ago.**

3. **Discuss the question at the end of the last paragraph.**

Review of units 1-4

1 ▶ Complete the paragraph with *when*, *as soon as*, *before*, and *after*.

My name's Tom Chomsky and I live in Apartment 44. I usually lead a very ordinary life. _when / as soon as_ I get up, I take a shower and get dressed. _as soon as / when_ the coffee is ready, I sit down and have breakfast. Then I usually go to work. _After / Before_ I leave the house, I get in my car and drive about half an hour. However, today I'm not going to work. _after_ I finish breakfast, I'm going downstairs to the pool. It's my birthday today—I'm twenty-eight years old—and I'm going to relax. Tonight some of my friends are having a party for me, so _before_ the stores close, I plan to go shopping for something new to wear.

2 ▶ Answer the questions with your own information.

1. What do you do as soon as you get up in the morning?
2. What do you do after you finish breakfast?
3. What do you usually do when you finish work or school?
4. What do you usually do in the evening before you go to bed?

3 ▶ Complete Tom's part of the conversation.

Alice You're in a good mood today.
Tom _____
Alice Oh, happy birthday! How old are you?
Tom _____
Alice And what are you going to do to celebrate your birthday?
Tom _____
Alice Well, have a good time.

I locked myself out of my house!
What am I going to do?
  You should ....   You could

locksmith

4 ▶ Choose *a* or *b* to complete the conversation.

Alice You look upset. Is anything wrong?
Tom a. Yes. I found my keys. They were in my apartment.
  ✓ b. Yes. I can't find my keys. I think I locked them in my apartment.
Alice Uh-oh. You've got a real problem because the building manager isn't here.
Tom ✓a. When will he be back?
  b. When did he leave?
Alice I don't know exactly. He went away for a week.
Tom ✓a. What am I going to do? I can't go to a party dressed like this.
  b. What are you going to do later?
Alice I don't know. But you're right. You can't go to a party dressed like that!
Tom a. Well, I'd better call the police. Maybe they can help.
  ✓ b. Well, I'd better get ready for the party. Maybe I'll go like this.

bathing suit
swimming suit
towel
sun hat

5 ▶ **Play these roles.**

Student A B locked his keys inside his apartment. Ask B what he is going to do about his keys. If you think his suggestion is good, tell him it's a good idea. If you don't think so, suggest something else he could do. Here are some possibilities:
(1) call a friend for help,
(2) climb in a window,
(3) borrow some clothes,
(4) not go to the party.

Student B You locked your keys inside your apartment. Tell A what you will do.
Here are some possibilities:
(1) call a friend for help,
(2) climb in a window,
(3) borrow some clothes for the party,
(4) not go to the party.

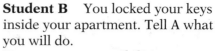

6 ▶ **Complete Tom's part of the conversation.**
▶ **Imagine you locked your keys in your car. Act out a similar conversation with a partner.**

Police	911. Where's the emergency?
Tom	_____
Police	What's your name?
Tom	_____
Police	And what's the problem?
Tom	_____
Police	Well, that's not really an emergency. Why don't you call a locksmith? He can open your door.
Tom	_____
Police	You're welcome.

  7 ▶ **Tom found a list of locksmiths in the telephone directory. Listen to the phone call and choose *a* or *b*.**

1. The name of the locksmith is
   a. A. B. Goode.
   ✓ b. AAA Locks.

2. The locksmith will be at Tom's apartment
   ✓ a. after lunch. ✓
   b. before lunch.

3. To unlock the apartment, it will cost
   a. $5.95 plus tax.
   ✓ b. $15.95 plus tax.

4. The phone call put Tom in a good mood because
   ✓ a. he can change his clothes for his birthday party.
   b. he can have a party in his apartment.

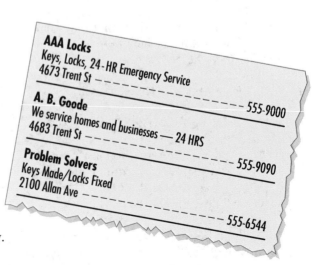

AAA Locks
Keys, Locks, 24-HR Emergency Service
4673 Trent St ————————— 555-9000

A. B. Goode
We service homes and businesses — 24 HRS
4683 Trent St ————————— 555-9090

Problem Solvers
Keys Made/Locks Fixed
2100 Allan Ave ————————— 555-6544

8 ▶ Tom's neighbors are talking. Complete each conversation, using a direct and an indirect object.

A We need to send that birthday card to Tom right away. His birthday is today.

B Don't worry. _I sent it to ~~Tom~~ him_ the day before yesterday.

A Hi. Could you give this package to Tom Chomsky in Apartment 44?

B Of course. _I will give it to him_ as soon as he comes home from work.

A Did we get any mail?

B No, only a letter for Tom Chomsky. The mail carrier _~~gave~~_ _____ by mistake.

~~did~~ delivered it to us

gave it to us

9A ▶ Student A follows the instructions below.
▶ Student B follows the instructions on page 46.

Student A You are going to Tom's birthday party, which is in an apartment building called Mason Towers. Ask your partner how far Mason Towers is and ask how you get there. Find Mason Towers on the map and thank your partner. Then give your partner directions to the place he or she asks about.

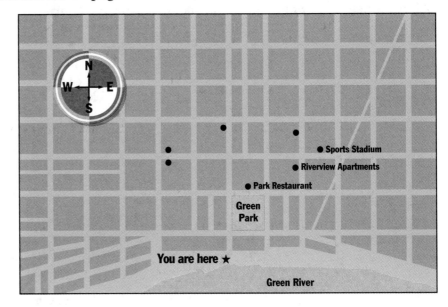

● Sports Stadium
● Riverview Apartments
● Park Restaurant
Green Park
You are here ★
Green River

10 ▶ You are at Tom's party and are talking to someone you don't know. Complete the conversation with your own information.

A _____
B I'm from Chicago originally.
A _____
B For only three months. Are you from here originally?
A _____
B Do you have any special interests?
A _____
B Me? Well, I like to read and go to the movies.

9B ► Student B follows the instructions below.
Student A follows the instructions on page 45.

Student B Look at the map and give your partner directions to the place he or she asks about. Then ask your partner how far the Sports Stadium is and ask how you get there. Find the Sports Stadium on the map and thank your partner.

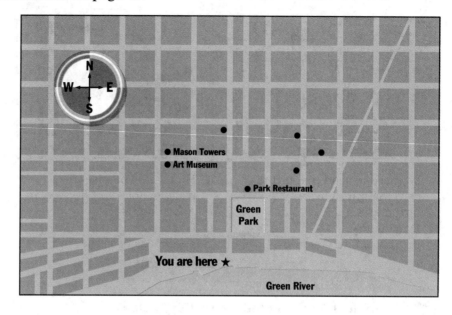

11 ► Imagine you have met someone interesting at Tom's party and want to see the person again. Put the conversation in order.
► Act out a similar conversation with a partner.

___ Fine.
___ No, I don't feel like seeing that. I don't like violent movies.
___ Maybe we could go to a movie or something this weekend.
___ Would you like to see *Lethal Weapon*?
___ Well, how about *Enchanted April*? The scenery's beautiful and it's very romantic.
___ That's a good idea. I love movies.

12 ► Complete the movie review with *someone* (*somebody*), *somewhere*, *something*, *anyone* (*anybody*), *anywhere*, *anything*, *no one* (*nobody*), *nowhere*, or *nothing*.

When you think about the title *Magic Adventure*, you think about fun, romance, good scenery, and perhaps even great music. But this movie didn't go *anywhere* exciting—the story was boring. In fact, I don't think there is *anything* positive I can say about *Magic Adventure*—there was *nothing* I liked about it.

The acting was terrible— *Nobody* seemed (No one) comfortable in the role he or she played—and the music wasn't special. I guess many other people agree with me because the movie theater was empty— *No one* was there! So, if you want to see *something* good—or *someone* in a good role—choose another movie.

13 ► Imagine you are buying two tickets for a movie and the cashier only gives you change for a ten-dollar bill. Act out the conversation with a partner.

A Two, please.
B _____
A Excuse me. I think I gave you a twenty.
B _____

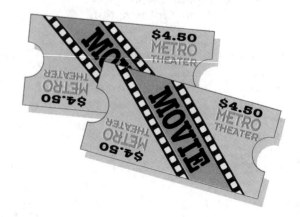

14 ► Talk with your classmates.

Tell your group the name of a movie you saw recently. Answer your classmates' questions.

P R E V I E W

FUNCTIONS/THEMES	LANGUAGE	FORMS
Suggest an alternative	Let's go to a baseball game. Why don't we go to a soccer game instead?	
Make a comparison	I like soccer better than baseball. The Grand Hotel isn't as expensive as the Ritz.	Comparisons with . . .*er than*, *more/less . . . than*, and *as . . . as*
Make a suggestion	Should we take some food with us? Yes. It's more expensive at the stadium.	*Should*
Talk about the weather State an expectation	What's the weather going to be like on Saturday? It's supposed to get colder. It's going to be cloudy too.	*Be supposed to*
Describe someone's appearance	What does your father look like? He's a little taller than I am. He's got curly brown hair, and he wears glasses.	*Look like*
Describe someone's personality	And what's he like? He's sort of quiet, but he's very nice.	*Be like*

Preview the conversations.

These people have been to a baseball game.
What spectator sports are popular in your
country? Do you ever go to these games?

The man on the left is tall. He
has brown hair and wears glasses.
Describe the man on the right.

24. I've got an idea.

— she is watering her garden

It's Saturday afternoon, and Patrick and Kate Shultz are making plans for the evening.

— I water my plants once a week.
— I watered my plants.

hoe ←

watering can   kerchief

fence →

wheelbarrow

A

Patrick I've got an idea. Let's go to a baseball game tonight.

Kate Why don't we go to a soccer game instead? I like soccer better than baseball.

Patrick Well, for one thing, it's not soccer season.

Kate Oh.

Patrick But the Angels are playing the Bulldogs tonight.

Kate Well, O.K. Uh . . . should we take some food with us?

Patrick Yes. It's more expensive at the stadium. By the way, what's the weather going to be like tonight?

Kate It's supposed to get cooler.

Patrick I hope so. It's really hot now. . . . Oh, there's the phone. I'll get it.

B

Patrick Kate, it's my cousin Ron. He's in town on business. Is it O.K. if I invite him to the game?

Kate Of course it's O.K.

Patrick Ron? Kate and I are going to the Angels game tonight. Would you like to come with us?

Ron Yeah. That'll be fun.

C

Patrick Do you remember Ron? He was at Bill's wedding. He's Aunt Sally's son.

Kate I don't think I met him. What does he look like?

Patrick Well, he's a little taller than I am, and he's got curly brown hair. And he wears glasses. I guess he's about thirty.

Kate No, I didn't meet him. What's he like?

Patrick He's a nice guy. He's sort of quiet, but he's got a good sense of humor.

Kate Where's he staying?

Patrick At the Ritz.

Kate Really? I'm surprised. The Grand is just as convenient as the Ritz, and it isn't as expensive.

D

Kate Well, Ron, what did you
think of the game?
Ron It was O.K.
Kate What did you think, Patrick?
Patrick I'm glad the Angels won,
but it wasn't as exciting as the
last game.

Figure it out

1. Listen to the conversations. Then say *True* or *False*.

1. Kate has met Patrick's cousin Ron before.
2. Kate, Patrick, and Ron went to a baseball game together. T

2. Listen again and choose *a* or *b*.

1. Kate likes
   a. baseball better than soccer.
   b. soccer better than baseball.

2. The food is
   a. more expensive at the stadium than at home.
   b. cheaper at the stadium than at home.

3. Ron is
   a. taller than Patrick.
   b. shorter than Patrick.

4. Patrick thinks
   a. the last game was more exciting.
   b. the last game was less exciting.

3. Match.

1. Should we take some food with us?
2. What's the weather going to be like?
3. There's the phone.
4. Is it O.K. if I invite him to the game?
5. Would you like to come with us?
6. What does he look like?
7. What's he like?
8. What did you think of the game?

a. Of course it's O.K.
b. He's sort of quiet.
c. I'll get it.
d. Yeah. That'll be fun.
e. It wasn't as exciting as the last game.
f. He's tall and wears glasses.
g. Yes. It's more expensive at the stadium.
h. It's supposed to get cooler.

25. Let's go to a baseball game.

1 ▶ **Listen to the conversation. Then circle *W* for the sports the woman prefers to see. Circle *M* for the sports the man prefers.**

Ⓦ M   W Ⓜ   Ⓦ M   Ⓦ M   W Ⓜ

1. A baseball game   2. A soccer game   3. A basketball game   4. A tennis match   5. A football game

2 ▶ **Listen to the conversations.**
▶ **Act out a similar conversation with a partner. Use the suggestions and comparisons in the box or your own ideas.**

A I've got an idea. Let's go to a baseball game.

B Why don't we go to a soccer game instead? I like soccer better than baseball.

A Well, O.K. Should we take some food with us?

B Yes. It's more expensive at the stadium.

B Yeah. That'll be fun. Should we take some food with us?

A Yes. It's more expensive at the stadium.

This pen is is big as this pen.

Some suggestions and comparisons	
Should we take . . .	Yes. It's . . .
the train?	faster than the bus.
some food?	more expensive at the stadium.
something to drink?	less expensive than at the stadium.
a jacket?	not as warm as yesterday.

3 ▶ **Study the frames: Comparisons with . . .*er than, more . . . than*, and *less . . . than***

The train is	**faster** **earlier**	**than**	the bus.	When an adjective or adverb is one syllable or ends in *y*, add *er*.

happier
thinner
hungrier
angrier
friendly
friendlier

Soccer is	**more** **less** exciting	**than**	baseball.	When an adjective or adverb has more than one syllable, use *more* or *less* + adjective or adverb.

Notice these spelling changes.

The bus arrived	**later** **earlier**	than the train.	late + *er* y → *ier*

The crowd was **bigger** than I expected.	When an adjective or adverb ends in a single vowel + a consonant, double the consonant before adding *er*.

Today's game was	**better** **worse**	than the one last week.	*Good* → *better* and *bad* → *worse* are irregular.

4 ▶ Complete the newspaper article with comparisons, using the words in parentheses.

Angels Win 7 to 4

With both teams playing very badly, last night's baseball game was certainly *less exciting than* (exciting) the last game. Angels pitcher Al Garcia's pitches were *slower than* (slow) usual, and the other players missed more balls than they caught. The weather didn't help either. It was much *colder than* (cold) it usually is at this time of year. The crowd was *more uncomfortable than* (uncomfortable) the players—the players were busy running and hitting and catching

balls—and many people left *earlier than* (early) normal because they didn't have jackets or sweaters. Two good things about baseball games this season: Tickets are *cheaper than* (cheap) last year, and the hot dogs and hamburgers seem *better* (good). And two bad things: Parking is *worse than* (bad) last year—there just aren't enough spaces for everyone—and the refreshments at the food stands are *more expensive* (expensive).

Angels pitcher Al Garcia

5 ▶ Study the frame: Comparisons with *as . . . as*

| The Grand | is just
isn't | **as** | **convenient**
expensive | **as** | the Ritz. |

Just in *just as . . . as* adds emphasis to the comparison and means "exactly."

6 ▶ Look at the travel brochure and compare the two hotels, using *just as . . . as* and *not as . . . as*. Then compare the bus and the train.

The Grand is just as convenient as the Ritz.

ACCOMMODATIONS

The Ritz Hotel
· is located on the corner of Island Boulevard and Grand Avenue.
· has 90 rooms.
· costs $125 for a room.

The Grand Hotel
· is located on the corner of Island Boulevard and Grand Avenue.
· has 240 rooms.
· costs $85 for a room.

Hotel

LOCAL TRANSPORTATION

The Bus
· takes 35 minutes to downtown.
· costs $1.25.
· is usually crowded.
· stops three blocks from International Plaza.

The Train
· takes 20 minutes to downtown.
· costs $1.25.
· is usually crowded.
· stops across the street from International Plaza.

7 ▶ Imagine you and a partner are planning a business trip. Decide where to stay and how to get to your appointments at International Plaza. Then tell the class which hotel and which form of transportation you think is better. Say why you think so.

26. It's supposed to get colder.

TALK ABOUT THE WEATHER • STATE AN EXPECTATION • *BE SUPPOSED TO*

 1 ▶ **Listen to the weekend weather report and choose *a* or *b*.**
  ▶ **Look at the weekend weather map in exercise 2 to check your work.**

1. On Saturday, it's supposed to be _____ in Los Angeles.
  ✓ a. warm and sunny
  b. sunny but cool

2. The temperature is supposed to be 72 degrees. That's about _____ degrees Celsius.
  a. 72
  ✓ b. 22

3. The weather in New York on Saturday is supposed to be _____ .
  a. sunny but cold
  ✓ b. rainy and cold

 2 ▶ **Listen to the conversation.**
  ▶ **Imagine you are in Los Angeles. Practice the conversation with a partner.**
  ▶ **Imagine you are in one of the other cities on the map and act out a similar conversation.**

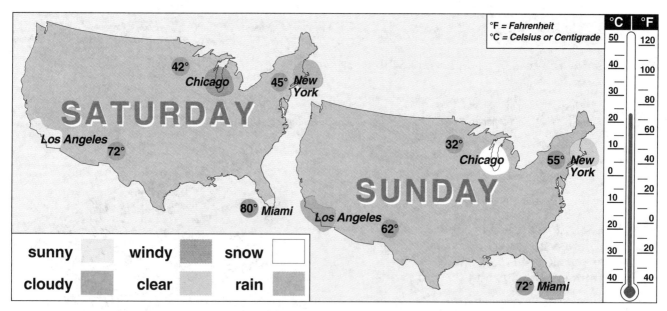

A What's the weather going to be like on Saturday?
B It's supposed to be warm and sunny.
A What about Sunday?
B It's supposed to get colder. It's going to be cloudy too.

activities *indoor / outdoor*
clothing *2 days*

It's supposed to . . .	
get be	cooler. colder. warmer. hotter. cloudy.
rain. snow. clear up.	

 3 ▶ **Talk to a classmate.**

Invite a classmate to do something after school, tonight, or this weekend. Answer your classmate's question about the weather.

A *Let's go to a soccer game tonight.*
B *That sounds like fun. What's the weather going to be like tonight?*
A *It's supposed to be nice.*

brush cut   braids
bangs   pony tail   tall/short   athlethic   hair-short-long
                           thin/fat   old/young   straight/curly   good sense of humor   agressive
                                                                                  generenous   angry
                                                                                  kind/helpful   funny / depressed
                                                                                                        sad/happy
                                                                                                        nervours/relaxed

27. What does he look like?

DESCRIBE SOMEONE'S APPEARANCE • *LOOK LIKE* • DESCRIBE SOMEONE'S PERSONALITY • *BE LIKE*

1 ▶ **Match the descriptions with the pictures.**

peaceful   friendly
~~extro~~   quiet

 1. k
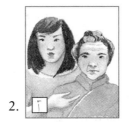 2. i
 3. a
 4. e
 5. ☐

 6. g
 7. b
 8. j
 9. d
 10. c

a. He's got curly brown hair.
b. She has short blond hair.
c. She's got long straight red hair.
d. He's bald.
e. He has a mustache.
f. He's got a beard.
g. She wears glasses.
h. He's taller than I am.
i. He's shorter than me.
j. She's about my height.

thin
works   2×2=
         9×9=0

2 ▶ **Listen to the conversation.**
▶ **Practice the conversation with a partner.**
▶ **Act out similar conversations. Ask your partner about a family member, a teacher, a boss, or someone else.**

A What does your father look like?
B He's a little taller than I am. He's got curly brown hair, and he wears glasses.
A And what's he like?
B He's sort of quiet, but he's very nice.

Some ways to describe personality

| She's He's | very really | friendly. outgoing. nice. easygoing. |
| | sort of a little | quiet. shy. moody. |

18×18=

3 ▶ **Henry, George, and Bill McDonald are brothers. Work with a partner and match each person with the correct description.**
▶ **Imagine you know Henry but not George or Bill. Ask questions about one of the other two brothers.**

I fast
I fasted yesterday.

___ 1.

___ 2.

___ 3.

a. Henry McDonald has blue eyes and curly black hair. He's about forty, and he wears glasses. He's very outgoing and has a great sense of humor too. He's a really nice guy.

b. George McDonald is a little younger than Henry, and he doesn't look like him at all. He's got curly light brown hair and a mustache. He's good-looking, but he probably should lose a little weight. He's less outgoing than Henry. In fact, he's a little shy.

c. Bill McDonald is a little older than Henry. He has curly black hair, and he's starting to go bald. He has a beard. He's a little moody and not as easygoing as Henry.

28. Would you like to see some pictures?

Emma, Tom, Steve, and Eva are at a rock concert. During the intermission, Eva shows everyone some pictures she took with her new camera.

1

Eva Wow! That was fantastic!

Steve Yeah. They were really incredible. I hope the second half is as good.

Emma Well, it was too loud for me. How about you, Tom?

Tom To tell you the truth, I don't really care for rock music.

Eva Well, we're all glad you came with us. Hey, would you like to see some pictures? I took them with my new camera.

Tom Sure.

Eva This is a picture of Steve's soccer team.

Steve The guy holding the ball is Charley, a good friend of mine.

Tom He's pretty tall.

Emma Actually, I think Charley and Steve are about the same height.

Steve No, Charley's a lot taller than I am.

Eva Anyway, here's a picture of my chemistry teacher, Miss Edwards.

Steve She looks very nice. What's she like?

Eva She's very smart, and she has a great personality. She's probably the best teacher in the school.

Steve Oh, look! Here comes the band. . . .

‹outdoor concert›

2. Figure it out

Say *True, False,* or *It doesn't say.*

1. Steve and Eva are really enjoying the concert. T.
2. Tom thought the band was too loud. F
3. Eva has a new camera. T
4. Eva took a picture of Steve's soccer team. T
5. Steve and Tom are about the same height. *doesn't say*
6. Eva doesn't like her chemistry teacher. F

3. Listen in

The young men above are listening to the weather forecast on the radio. Read the statements below. Then listen to the weather forecast and choose *a* or *b.*

1. The temperature in Los Angeles today is
   a. eighty degrees.
   b. seventy-four degrees.

2. Tonight, it's supposed to get
   a. a little cooler.
   b. a lot warmer.

4. How to say it

Practice the conversation.

A Tennis is more exciting than baseball.

B Yes, but soccer is more exciting than tennis.

A Oh, I think tennis is as exciting as soccer.

B Well, I like soccer better than tennis.

5. Your turn

After the rock concert, Steve invites Eva to come to his apartment and watch television. Act out the conversation. Use the information below.

Steve invites Eva to come to his apartment and watch television.	Eva accepts Steve's invitation to go to his apartment and watch television.
He wants to watch a baseball game on television.	She wants to watch a tennis match on television.
He'd like to make a chicken dinner with rice and vegetables to have while he and Eva watch the game.	She wants to eat dinner while they watch the game, too. But she'd like to go to a fast-food restaurant and get some fried chicken and french fries to go. *takeout order bring food back*
He'd also like to invite Charley to come over and watch television with them.	She feels tired. She would like to have a quiet evening with her brother and go home early.

ROCK

29.

It's everywhere. It's on the radio, our stereos, and Walkmans. Turn on the TV and you will probably find a station that plays rock music videos. Rock first became popular in the 1950s in the United States. Called "rock 'n' roll," it developed from a variety of different styles of music—for example, jazz, blues, and church gospel singing. Here are only a few of the many performers and groups that have made rock popular around the world.

1950s

With his first hit "Tutti Frutti," **Little Richard** demonstrated a wild and exciting style of performing that influenced many later rock performers.

Chuck Berry was the first of the great rock songwriters and his first hit record was "Maybellene." Many performers, including Elvis Presley and the Beatles, said Berry influenced their own music.

"Rock Around the Clock" by **Bill Haley and the Comets** was the first international rock hit and is still one of the best-selling records of all time.

Elvis Presley had a huge success with "Heartbreak Hotel" in 1956. Elvis went on to become one of the biggest superstars in the history of popular music.

1960s

In the 1960s, the **Beatles** were the first of many groups from England to become famous around the world. One of their first major hits was "I Want to Hold Your Hand."

Another British group that is still popular today is the **Rolling Stones**. The "Stones" showed the influence of blues in their music, and one of their hit songs was "I Can't Get No Satisfaction."

Bob Dylan sang songs about problems in the world like war and poverty. Because of his roots in folk music, his style became known as folk rock. A popular Dylan song is "Blowin' in the Wind."

Music by black singers like **Diana Ross and the Supremes** came from Detroit, Michigan, and became known as soul music. "Stop in the Name of Love" was one of their hits.

1970s

Led Zeppelin ("Stairway to Heaven") was one of the popular "heavy metal" groups of the day. Heavy metal was influenced by 60s musicians like Jimi Hendrix who experimented with the electric guitar.

Although some critics feel that rock in the 70s lost the spirit and excitement of the music of the 50s and 60s, **Bruce Springsteen** demonstrated some of the youthful energy of the previous two decades with such songs as "Born to Run" and "Thunder Road."

Reggae—the music made famous by **Bob Marley** from the Caribbean nation Jamaica—brought a new sound to rock. A popular example was the song "Stir It Up."

Donna Summer ("Last Dance") became known as the Queen of Disco. Disco music was often influenced by rhythms from Latin America.

1980s

Run D.M.C. was one of the first successful rap groups. Rap performers "talk" rather than sing the words of songs about the worries and problems of young people in a tough world.

Rock videos opened the eyes as well as the ears to music and dance. **Madonna**, one of rock's superstars, became famous for her recordings, videos, and live performances.

Michael Jackson is another name that is known all over the world. His album *Thriller* became the biggest-selling record album of all time.

Peter Gabriel and **Tracy Chapman** were among the many artists who gave concerts to promote social change in the United States and around the world.

Read the article and answer the questions.

1. Without looking at the article, name one important singer or group from the 1950s, the 1960s, the 1970s, and the 1980s.

2. Can you name any other major singers or groups that should be included in each decade?

3. What singers or groups are popular in this decade?

FUNCTIONS/THEMES	LANGUAGE	FORMS
Request permission formally	May I use your phone? Certainly.	*May*
Report a lost item	I lost my passport.	
Ask for and show identification	Do you have any identification? Yes. Here's a credit card.	
Thank someone	Thank you very much. Don't mention it.	
Give advice	Just be more careful next time.	
Describe a car accident Provide information	What happened exactly? A car went through the red light. I slammed on the brakes and went off the road. Can you describe the other car? I think it was a Ford Escort. What color was it? Dark blue. Did you get the license plate number? No, I didn't.	
Express sympathy Wish someone well Say what you think	I'm sorry (that) you wrecked your car. I hope (that) your car is O.K. I think (that) you're very lucky.	*That* + noun clause
Talk about an accident	Who has had an accident? I have. What happened? I was on my bike and a car hit me.	Review: subject questions and short answers

Preview the conversations.

Have you ever had a car accident? What happened?
Did the police come to the scene of the accident?

30. Accident

Eric and Michelle are driving home from a weekend in the country.

A

Police officer Who's the driver of the car?
Eric I am.
Police officer May I see your driver's license, please?
Eric Yes. Here you are.
Police officer What happened exactly?
Eric Well, a car went through the red light. I slammed on the brakes, and my car went off the road and hit the sign.
Police officer Did the other driver stop?
Eric No, he didn't. He didn't even slow down.
Police officer All right. Could you come back to my car? I have to fill out a report.

B

Police officer Miss, could I have your name, please? I'm listing you as a witness.
Michelle Michelle Kelley. K-E-L-L-E-Y.
Police officer Do you have any identification?
Michelle Yes. Here's my driver's license.

 C

Police officer Can you describe the other car?

Eric I don't really remember what it looked like.

Michelle Hmm . . . it was a small car. I think it was a Ford Escort.

Police officer What color was it?

Michelle Dark blue.

Police officer Did you get the license plate number?

Michelle No, I didn't.

Eric Neither did I. We're just glad that we didn't get hurt—or <u>wreck</u> our car.

Police officer Yeah. Well, it's a good thing you had your seat belts on.

D

Police officer All right. I think I have all the information I need.

Eric May we go now?

Police officer Sure. . . . I hope your car is O.K.

Eric Thanks. I think there's just a dent in the front.

Police officer Well, just be more careful next time.

Eric Don't worry. We will.

Figure it out

1. Listen to the conversations and choose the correct answer.

a. The accident was Eric's fault.
b. The accident was the other driver's fault.

2. Listen again. Then say *True, False,* or *It doesn't say*.

1. Eric is the driver of the car.
2. He has a driver's license.
3. The driver of the other car also has a driver's license.
4. The other car stopped at the red light.
5. The other driver was a woman.
6. Michelle saw the other driver.
7. Eric's car has a dent in the front.

3. Find another way to say it.

1. Who's driving the car?
2. Give me your driver's license, please.
3. How did it happen?
4. Come back to my car, please.
5. Tell me your name, please.
6. What did the other car look like?
7. Can we go now?

31. May I use your phone?

1 ▶ Complete the exchanges with the requests in the box.
▶ Listen to check your work.
▶ Practice the exchanges with a partner.

May I borrow your pen?	May I go to the restroom?
May I use your phone?	May I have your name?
May I join you?	May I look at your newspaper?

Karras. Robert Karras.

1

May I use your phone?

Certainly.

2

May I borrow your pen

May I look at your newspaper

Of course.

3

May I go to the restroom

No, you may not. You just went five minutes ago!

4

You may have it. I've finished reading it.

5

May I from you

Of course. I hate to eat alone.

6

2 ▶ Study the frame: *May*

	I		Yes,	you	**may.**
	he			he	
May	she	**use** your phone?		she	
	we		No,	you	**may not.**
	they			they	

In most situations, it is more common to give a reason than to say "may not."

May I use your phone?
No. I'm sorry. I need to use it right now.

3 ▶ Talk to a classmate.

Imagine you need a pen, a piece of paper, or some other item. Request permission from a classmate to borrow or use the item.

In Moby-Dick Captain Ahab seeks revenge on the ...

32. Do you have any identification?

REPORT A LOST ITEM • ASK FOR AND SHOW IDENTIFICATION • THANK SOMEONE • GIVE ADVICE

1 ▶ Listen to the conversation. Then circle the
numbers of the items the woman lost.

– photo ID

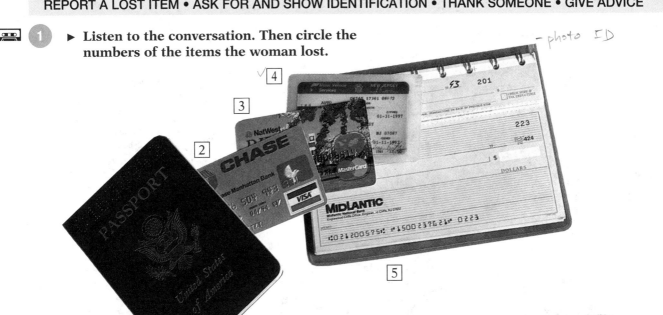

2 ▶ Listen to the two possible conversations.
▶ Act out the conversations with a partner,
using your own name.

A May I help you?
B Yes. I lost my passport.
A What's your name?
B Dorothy Foster.

A Just one second. . . . Yes. We have
it. Do you have any identification?

B Yes. Here's a credit card.

A O.K. Here you are. Just sign
here, please.

B Thank you very much.

A Don't mention it. Just be more careful next time.

B Don't worry. I will.

A Just one second. . . . No. I'm sorry, we don't
have it. Why don't you check again in a few days?

B O.K., I will. Thank you.

3 ▶ Play these roles.

Student A Imagine you are a police officer at a police station. A tourist has come in to
report something he or she lost. Offer assistance, find out the tourist's name, and return
the lost item to the tourist. Be sure to ask for identification and to have the tourist sign
for the item.

Student B Imagine you are a tourist in another city. You are at the police station
because you have lost something. Tell the police officer what you lost and answer the
officer's questions. Be prepared to show some identification—a driver's license, a
passport, or some credit cards.

33. What happened?

  ▶ **Listen and match each conversation with the picture it describes.**

  ▶ **Listen to the two possible conversations with the police officer.**
▶ **Act out a similar conversation with a partner.**

Officer	Who's the driver of this car?
Man	I am.
Officer	What happened exactly?
Man	A car went through a red light. I slammed on the brakes and went off the road.
Officer	Can you describe the other car?

Man	Yes. It was a small car. I think it was a Ford Escort.	**Man**	No. I don't really remember what it looked like.
Officer	What color was it?	**Officer**	Did you get the license plate number?
Man	Dark blue.	**Man**	No, I didn't.
Officer	Did you get the license plate number?		
Man	Yes. It was XYZ 93M.		

Some things that happen when you are driving

A car	went through the red light. went off the road. ran into the tree. backed into me. There was a dog in the middle of the road.	I slammed on the brakes and	skidded into the motorcycle. hit the car in front of me. ran into the tree. went off the road. tried to miss the dog.

3
► Listen to the conversation.
► Imagine your partner told you that he or she had one of the accidents described in exercise 1. Act out a similar conversation. Make an appropriate comment to end the conversation.

A I just had an accident.
B What happened?
A I ran into a tree and wrecked my car.
B I'm sorry you wrecked your car, but I'm glad you didn't get hurt.
A Yeah. It's a good thing I had my seat belt on.
B Well, I think you're very lucky.

Some comments			
Express sympathy	I'm sorry It's too bad		you wrecked your car. you got hurt.
Wish someone well	I hope I'm glad	(that)	your car is O.K. it wasn't serious.
Say what you think	I think I guess I imagine		you're very lucky. you'll be more careful next time. you were pretty scared.

That is optional and is often omitted, especially in speech.

TALK ABOUT AN ACCIDENT • REVIEW: SUBJECT QUESTIONS AND SHORT ANSWERS

4
► Study the frame: Review of subject questions and short answers

Subject questions are always asked with a singular verb.

Who knows what happened?	I do.
Who's the driver of this car?	I am.
Who's responsible for the accident?	They are.
Who can tell me about the accident?	He can.
Who else was in the car?	She was.
Who saw the accident?	I did.
Who has had a car accident?	Eric (has).
What hit you?	A truck (did).

When the answer is a noun, auxiliaries such as *is, was, do, did,* and *has* are optional.

5
► Work in a group and ask your classmates about accidents they have had. You can use the questions in exercise 4 or your own questions. Make comments like the ones in exercise 3 when appropriate.

A *Who has had an accident?*
B *I have.*
C *What happened?*
B *I was on my bike and a car hit me.*
D *. . .*

34. You look familiar.

Stacy Edwards is on her way to school when she sees steam coming from under the hood of her car. She gets off the freeway and goes to a garage near the exit.

1

Stacy	Could you help me, please?
Steve	Sure. What's the trouble?
Stacy	I think the radiator exploded. The engine probably overheated.
Steve	Let me take a look.
Stacy	I hope you can fix it.
Steve	(*Looks under hood*) Well, I don't think I can today. I'll probably have to order a new radiator for it.
Stacy	You mean I can't use my car?
Steve	No, I'm afraid not. . . . Say, you look familiar.
Stacy	So do you.
Steve	My name's Steve Kovacs.
Stacy	Kovacs? Do you have a younger sister named Eva?
Steve	Yes, I do.
Stacy	She's a student of mine.
Steve	Oh, then you must be Miss Edwards, her chemistry teacher.
Stacy	Yes, I am. I'm glad to meet you.
Steve	Glad to meet you, too. So, can I give you a ride somewhere?
Stacy	Well, I don't know. Are you sure it's no trouble?
Steve	No, not at all.
Stacy	Well, thanks. I appreciate it. I really have to get to school.

2. Figure it out

Say *True, False,* or *It doesn't say.*

1. Stacy's car overheated.
2. Stacy drove into Steve's repair shop.
3. Steve can fix her car today.
4. Stacy has to buy a new radiator.
5. Stacy looks familiar to Steve because they have met before.
6. Stacy's going to take the bus to school tomorrow.

3. Listen in

A woman has come to pick up her car. Read the questions below. Then listen to the conversation and answer the questions.

1. How much does the woman have to pay?
2. What kinds of identification does she have?

4. How to say it

Practice the conversation.

A Who's the owner of this car?

B I am.

A It's such an old car.

B It really is.

5. Your turn

John Wilson had a car accident a few days ago, and he brings his car to Steve's shop. Steve and Bob are out to lunch, so Margaret asks him what happened. Play the roles below.

Margaret   Ask John how the accident happened. Find out about the other car and the driver. Also, ask John what the police did.

John   Describe how your car was hit on the freeway on your way to work. After the accident, you talked to the driver of the other car and found out she wasn't hurt. The police soon came and made a complete report.

35.

A horseless carriage, 1892

Air conditioning, ABS, and air bags are common in today's cars.

In-car computers will provide information about traffic and road conditions.

There have been many changes in the automobile since the introduction of the first "horseless carriage." Among other things, we have seen the addition of power steering, power windows, air conditioning, anti-lock brake systems (ABS), and air bags to protect the driver and passenger in case of an accident. A car can even have a telephone if the buyer can afford it.

Today, automobile companies are trying to develop cars that use less gasoline—and cause less pollution. The state of California passed a law which says that by the year 2003, ten percent of the cars sold in that state should make no exhaust pollution. Consequently, there is a great deal of interest in developing a good electric car. Models of these cars—cars that make no noise and run on batteries—already exist.

Using computer technology, automobile companies and local governments are also experimenting with information systems that join together cars, highways, and central information centers: a computer in the car "reads" sensors on the road and sends information to a central area. Information about traffic and road conditions is then sent back to the in-car computer. Also, the in-car computer can help drivers figure out where they are, and how to get to their destination as easily as possible. These systems, called Intelligent Vehicle/Highway Systems (IVHS), are already being tested in cities in the United States, Japan, and certain countries in Europe.

According to *Popular Mechanics* magazine, one day highway travel will be automated from the time you get on a highway until you get off. A driver "will simply push a button on the computer inside the car and choose his destination. The computer will then find the fastest way to, say, the office, taking into account information about current traffic." The driver will still have to drive the car on local streets. However, once the driver is on a major highway or expressway, the car will drive itself.

1. Read the article. Then match the underlined words with their definitions.

1. carriage
2. pollution
3. sensor
4. destination
5. be automated
6. taking into account

a. something that is used to "read" the quantity of light, sound, noise, etc.
b. the place where you are going
c. considering
d. dirt and chemicals in the air that are not good for people
e. work without the help of people
f. a vehicle that is usually pulled by horses

2. Answer the questions.

1. What does IVHS stand for?
2. How does IVHS work?
3. Choose the best title for the article.
   a. From the Horseless Carriage to the Intelligent Car
   b. Cars that Run on Batteries and Make No Noise
   c. Today's Traffic Problems

PREVIEW

FUNCTIONS/THEMES	LANGUAGE	FORMS
Talk about plans	What are you doing this weekend? I'm not sure yet. Why? I think I'll have some people over for dinner.	Review: the future with *going to*, the present continuous as future, and the future with *will*
Invite someone	My parents are having a barbecue on Sunday. Would you like to come? O.K. That sounds nice.	
Offer to bring something	Can I bring anything? Oh, no. We already have everything we need. I could bring something to drink. Well, if you want to, but you really don't have to.	
Offer help Accept or decline help	Would you like some help with that? Oh, thanks. No, thanks. I can manage.	
Introduce yourself	You're Rick's friend, aren't you? Yes, I am. I'm Tracy, Rick's sister.	Tag questions
Continue a conversation	So, how do you know Rick? We go to school together.	
Talk about things in common	Carol works at ABC Industries. So does Tracy. Carol isn't going to school full time. Neither is Tracy.	Rejoinders with *so* and *neither*
Say good-bye to a host	You're not leaving already, are you? Yes. I have to go. But I want to thank you for everything. Well, I'm glad you could come. So am I. I enjoyed myself very much.	

Preview the conversations.

When you are invited to a barbecue, dinner, or a party at someone's home in the United States, it is very common to take something to your host or hostess—perhaps a bottle of wine, some candy, or some flowers. Is this common in your country?

36. Barbecue

Matt Rubino and Ted Harwood work for Atlas Window Cleaners in Chicago. They're talking about their plans for the weekend.

A

Ted What are you doing this weekend, Matt?

Matt I'm not sure yet. Why?

Ted Well, my parents are having a barbecue on Sunday. Would you like to come?

Matt Are you sure it's O.K.? Your parents don't know me.

Ted Of course. They always like to meet my friends. Some of my sister's friends will be there, too. It'll be a lot of fun.

Matt O.K. That sounds nice. Can I bring anything?

Ted Oh, no. We already have everything we need.

Matt I could bring something to drink.

Ted Well, if you want to, but you really don't have to.

B

Matt Would you like some help with that?
Susan Oh, thanks. You're Ted's friend, aren't you?
Matt Yes, I am.
Susan I'm Susan, Ted's sister.
Matt It's nice to meet you. I'm Matt.
Susan So, how do you know Ted?
Matt We work together.
Susan You mean at Atlas Window Cleaners?
Matt Yeah.
Susan Do you like the work? It seems dangerous.
Matt It's O.K. It's just a temporary job.
Susan Oh? What are you planning to do?
Matt Well, I'd like to be a computer programmer.
In fact, I just registered for a computer training
course at Elmhurst College.
Susan What a coincidence! So did I. Are you
taking the intensive program?
Matt No. I work all day, so I don't have the time.
Susan Neither do I. I'm taking evening classes.
Matt Well, maybe we'll be in the same class.

C

Ted's mother You're not leaving already, are you?
Matt Yes. I have to. But I want to thank you
for everything.
Ted's mother Well, we're glad you could come.
Matt So am I. I enjoyed myself very much.
Ted's mother Good. I hope you'll come
again soon.
Matt Thank you.

Figure it out

1. Listen to the conversations. Then choose *a* or *b*.

1. a. Susan is Ted's sister. ✓
   b. Susan is Matt's sister.

2. a. Susan and Matt work together.
   b. Ted and Matt work together. ✓

3. a. Susan and Ted are both going to study at Elmhurst College.
   b. Susan and Matt are both going to study at Elmhurst College. ✓

2. Listen again and say *True, False,* or *It doesn't say.*

1. Ted's family is having a barbecue this weekend. ✓ T
2. Ted's parents know Matt. False
3. Susan is Ted's younger sister. T
4. Matt wants to take something to drink to the barbecue. T
5. Both Matt and Susan are taking a computer
   training course. T
6. Matt had a good time at the barbecue. T

3. Find another way to say it.

1. I don't know yet.
2. Sure.
3. Are you Ted's friend?
4. I did too.
5. I don't either.
6. I had a good time.

37. Can I bring anything?

  1 ▶ Listen to the conversation between Nancy and Andrew. Then answer the questions below.
▶ What are some other things people do on the weekend?

1. What are Andrew and his girlfriend doing on Saturday? What are they going to do on Sunday?
2. What are Nancy and her boyfriend doing on Saturday? What are they going to do on Sunday?

  2 ▶ Listen to the conversation.
▶ Imagine you don't have any plans this weekend. Act out a similar conversation, accepting your partner's invitation. Use the plans in the boxes or your own ideas.

A What are you doing this weekend?
B I'm not sure yet. Why?
A My parents are having a barbecue on Sunday. Would you like to come?
B Are you sure it's O.K.?
A Of course. It'll be a lot of fun.
B O.K. That sounds nice.

Some plans

My parents are having a barbecue.

I think I'll have some people over for dinner.

I'm planning a surprise birthday party for my sister.

My girlfriend and I are having a picnic.

My husband and I are going to the beach.

My roommate and I are having a party.

  3 ▶ Listen to the rest of the conversation in exercise 2.
▶ Have a similar conversation with a partner.

B Can I bring anything?
A Oh, no. We already have everything we need.
B I could bring something to drink.
A Well, if you want to, but you really don't have to.

I could bring . . .	
some wine.	something to drink.
some candy.	something to eat.
some flowers.	something for dessert.

4 ▶ **Study the frames.**

Review: The future with *going to*, the present continuous as future, and the future with *will*

What **are** you	**doing going to do**	after work?		We're	**going going to go**	to a movie.
			Maybe	we'll	**go**	

My parents **are going to have** a barbecue on Sunday. My parents **are having** a barbecue on Sunday.	The future with *going to* and with the present continuous are used to talk about plans and intentions that we have thought about before the moment of speaking.
I**'ll see** you tomorrow. I**'ll call** you soon. I hope you**'ll go** with me.	*Will* is used when we decide something at the moment of speaking.
Maybe I**'ll come** later. I**'ll probably come** later. I think I**'ll come** later.	*Will* is often used to talk about things that are possible but not certain.
I**'ll give** him the message for you. I**'ll have** the fried chicken.	*Will* is also used to offer help and to make requests.

5 ▶ **Complete the conversation with an appropriate form of the future and the verbs in parentheses.**

A What ___are___ you ___doing___ (do) this weekend?

B Oh, no! Did I forget to tell you? I ___'m having___ (have) a picnic . . . on Saturday.

A Yes, you forgot. So, who ___will come___ (come) to your picnic?

B Oh, I invited all of my neighbors. A few friends from school ___will come___ (come), too.

A What about Victor and Maura?

B Oh, I forgot all about them too. And I don't have their phone number.

A I ___'ll ask___ (ask) them for you. I ___'ll see___ (see) them tonight.

B Oh, thanks.

A Can I bring anything?

B No, I have everything.

A I ___could bring___ (bring) some soda.

B Well, if you want to. So, I ___will see___ (see) you on Saturday.

A Yeah. I think I ___will come___ (come) early in case you forget something else!

B Uh . . . thanks. I appreciate it.

6 ▶ **Find out what a classmate is going to do this weekend. If appropriate, invite your classmate to join you in one of your weekend activities.**

38. You're Rick's friend, aren't you?

 1
- ► Complete the exchanges with the offers in the box.
- ► Listen to check your work.
- ► Practice the exchanges with a partner.

Would you like some help with those chairs? | Would you like help with the kids?
Would you like help with the fire? | Would you like some help with the salad?

No, thanks. I can manage.

Oh, thank you.

1

Oh, thanks. You can cut the tomatoes.

2

Sure.

3

4

 2
- ► Listen to the conversation between Adam and Tracy.
- ► Imagine you are at the picnic in exercise 1. Have a similar conversation with a partner. Use your own information.

Adam Would you like some help with that?
Tracy Oh, thanks. You're Rick's friend, aren't you?
Adam Yes, I am.
Tracy I'm Tracy, Rick's sister.
Adam It's nice to meet you. I'm Adam.
Tracy So, how do you know Rick?
Adam We go to school together.

Some ways you might know someone
We go to school together.
We used to work together.
We met at a party.
I met him through a friend.

 3
- ► Study the frames: Tag questions

I'm late as usual, **aren't I**?	Yes, you are.
I'm not late, **am I**?	No, you aren't.
You're Rick's friend, **aren't you**?	Yes, I am.
You aren't in my class, **are you**?	No, I'm not.
He's having fun, **isn't he**?	Yes, he is.
The weather isn't very nice, **is it**?	No, it isn't.
You know my brother, **don't you**?	Yes, I do.
He doesn't know my sister, **does he**?	No, he doesn't.

We often add a tag question to a statement when we want to confirm the information in the statement: *I'm late, aren't I? Yes, you are.* However, you could also disagree and answer "No, you aren't."

Notice the irregular tag *aren't I?*

TAG QUESTIONS • CONTINUE A CONVERSATION

  4 ▶ **Complete the conversation with tag questions.**
▶ **Listen to check your work.**

Carol You're one of Rick's friends, _aren't you_ ?
Tracy I'm his sister. Who are you?
Carol My name's Carol Rousseau.
Tracy You're not Claude's wife, _are you_ ?
Carol Yeah. How do you know Claude?
Tracy I don't really. He always calls Rick
when he needs help with his homework.
He doesn't like to study much, _does_ ? _he_

Carol No, he really doesn't.
Tracy Rousseau. That's a French name, _isn't it_ ?
Carol Uh-huh. Claude was born in Quebec.
Tracy But you don't come from Canada, _do you_ ?
Carol No. I'm from here.

TALK ABOUT THINGS IN COMMON • REJOINDERS WITH *SO* AND *NEITHER*

 5 ▶ **Listen to the conversation. Check (√) the things Carol and Tracy have in common.**

Carol and Tracy
____ work at ABC Industries.
____ don't work in a factory.
____ are going to quit their jobs.
____ registered for a computer training course.

Carol and Tracy
____ are taking classes at night.
____ aren't going to school full time.
____ will be in Computers 101.
____ love school.

6 ▶ **Look at the chart in exercise 5. Make comments about Carol and Tracy.**

A *Carol works at ABC.*
B *So does Tracy.*
C *Carol doesn't work in a factory.*
D *Neither does Tracy.*

Some rejoinders	
So does Tracy.	= Tracy does too.
Neither did Tracy.	= Tracy didn't either.
So is Tracy.	= Tracy is too.
Neither was Tracy.	= Tracy wasn't either.
So will Tracy.	= Tracy will too.
Neither can Tracy.	= Tracy can't either.

7 ▶ **Talk to a classmate.**

Imagine you are meeting your classmate for the first time at a picnic or party. Find out about your classmate. You can ask some of the questions below or questions of your own. If appropriate, use rejoinders to provide information about yourself.

Where do you go to school?
Do you go full time or part time?
Are you in the intensive program?
What class are you in?

How do you like your classes?
Where did you study before?
Do you think you'll register for another course here?
What would you like to do when you finish?

SAY GOOD-BYE TO A HOST

  8 ▶ **Listen to the conversation.**
▶ **Imagine you are at a party and have to leave. Say good-bye to your host or hostess.**

A You're not leaving already, are you?
B Yes. I have to go. But I want to thank you for everything.
A Well, I'm glad you could come.
B So am I. I enjoyed myself very much.

39. Congratulations!

Steve has invited Stacy Edwards to see a movie. They're supposed to meet Charley and his friend J.J. in front of the movie theater.

1

Steve	I wonder where Charley and J.J. are. The movie's going to start soon, isn't it?
Stacy	Oh, they'll probably be here in a few minutes. By the way, what does J.J. stand for?
Steve	Oh, Jennifer something. I can't remember. . . . I think you'll like her. She's studying biology at UCLA. . . . Oh, here they are.
Charley	Hi, everybody.
Steve	Hi. Stacy, I'd like you to meet Charley and J.J.
J.J.	Nice to meet you.
Charley	Yes, nice to meet you. We've heard a lot about you from Steve and Eva.
Stacy	Nothing bad, I hope.
J.J.	Oh, no. Only good things.
Charley	Sorry we're late. I had a job interview after work, and it took longer than I thought.
J.J.	He kept me waiting too.
Steve	So, tell us about the interview.
Charley	I got the job. I'm going to teach physical education at Walt Whitman High School. . . . And I'm going to coach the soccer team!
Steve	Hey, that's terrific. Congratulations!
Charley	Yeah, I can't believe it. I'm finally going to get paid for doing something I like.

2. Figure it out

Put the events in the right order.

____ Charley and J.J. met Stacy and Steve at the movie theater.
____ Charley had a job interview.
____ Charley told Stacy and Steve about the job.
____ Steve introduced Stacy to J.J. and Charley.
____ A school offered Charley a job as soccer coach and he took it.
____ Steve congratulated Charley.
____ Charley picked up J.J. to go to the movie.

39. Congratulations!

Steve has invited Stacy Edwards to see a movie. They're supposed to meet Charley and his friend J.J. in front of the movie theater.

1

Steve	I wonder where Charley and J.J. are. The movie's going to start soon, isn't it?
Stacy	Oh, they'll probably be here in a few minutes. By the way, what does J.J. stand for?
Steve	Oh, Jennifer something. I can't remember. . . . I think you'll like her. She's studying biology at UCLA. . . . Oh, here they are.
Charley	Hi, everybody.
Steve	Hi. Stacy, I'd like you to meet Charley and J.J.
J.J.	Nice to meet you.
Charley	Yes, nice to meet you. We've heard a lot about you from Steve and Eva.
Stacy	Nothing bad, I hope.
J.J.	Oh, no. Only good things.
Charley	Sorry we're late. I had a job interview after work, and it took longer than I thought.
J.J.	He kept me waiting too.
Steve	So, tell us about the interview.
Charley	I got the job. I'm going to teach physical education at Walt Whitman High School. . . . And I'm going to coach the soccer team!
Steve	Hey, that's terrific. Congratulations!
Charley	Yeah, I can't believe it. I'm finally going to get paid for doing something I like.

2. Figure it out

Put the events in the right order.

____ Charley and J.J. met Stacy and Steve at the movie theater.
____ Charley had a job interview.
____ Charley told Stacy and Steve about the job.
____ Steve introduced Stacy to J.J. and Charley.
____ A school offered Charley a job as soccer coach and he took it.
____ Steve congratulated Charley.
____ Charley picked up J.J. to go to the movie.

TAG QUESTIONS • CONTINUE A CONVERSATION

  4 ▶ Complete the conversation with tag questions.
▶ Listen to check your work.

Carol You're one of Rick's friends, _aren't you_ ?
Tracy I'm his sister. Who are you?
Carol My name's Carol Rousseau.
Tracy You're not Claude's wife, _are you_ ?
Carol Yeah. How do you know Claude?
Tracy I don't really. He always calls Rick when he needs help with his homework. He doesn't like to study much, _does_ ? _he_

Carol No, he really doesn't.
Tracy Rousseau. That's a French name, _isn't it_ ?
Carol Uh-huh. Claude was born in Quebec.
Tracy But you don't come from Canada, _do you_ ?
Carol No. I'm from here.

TALK ABOUT THINGS IN COMMON • REJOINDERS WITH SO AND NEITHER

 5 ▶ Listen to the conversation. Check (√) the things Carol and Tracy have in common.

Carol and Tracy	Carol and Tracy
___ work at ABC Industries.	___ are taking classes at night.
___ don't work in a factory.	___ aren't going to school full time.
___ are going to quit their jobs.	___ will be in Computers 101.
___ registered for a computer training course.	___ love school.

6 ▶ Look at the chart in exercise 5. Make comments about Carol and Tracy.

A *Carol works at ABC.*
B *So does Tracy.*
C *Carol doesn't work in a factory.*
D *Neither does Tracy.*

Some rejoinders		
So does Tracy.	=	Tracy does too.
Neither did Tracy.	=	Tracy didn't either.
So is Tracy.	=	Tracy is too.
Neither was Tracy.	=	Tracy wasn't either.
So will Tracy.	=	Tracy will too.
Neither can Tracy.	=	Tracy can't either.

 7 ▶ Talk to a classmate.

Imagine you are meeting your classmate for the first time at a picnic or party. Find out about your classmate. You can ask some of the questions below or questions of your own. If appropriate, use rejoinders to provide information about yourself.

Where do you go to school?
Do you go full time or part time?
Are you in the intensive program?
What class are you in?

How do you like your classes?
Where did you study before?
Do you think you'll register for another course here?
What would you like to do when you finish?

SAY GOOD-BYE TO A HOST

  8 ▶ Listen to the conversation.
▶ Imagine you are at a party and have to leave. Say good-bye to your host or hostess.

A You're not leaving already, are you?
B Yes. I have to go. But I want to thank you for everything.
A Well, I'm glad you could come.
B So am I. I enjoyed myself very much.

▄▄ 3. Listen in

Steve, Stacy, Charley, and J.J. discuss the movie as they leave the theater. Each one has a different opinion of the movie. Read the opinions below. Then listen to their conversation and match each person with his or her opinion.

1. The movie was boring.   a. Charley
2. The movie was O.K.   b. J.J.
3. The movie was pretty good.   c. Stacy
4. The movie was terrific.   d. Steve

▄▄ 4. How to say it

Practice the conversations.

1. **A** I didn't like the movie at all.

   B Neither did I.

   A I thought it was really boring.

   B So did I.

2. **A** You're Charley's friend, aren't you?

   B Yes, I am.

   A You aren't leaving already, are you?

   B Yes, I have to.

   A Oh, come on. You don't have to leave so soon, do you?

   B Yes, I really do.

5. Your turn

Charley and J.J. are saying good-bye to Steve and Stacy. Act out the conversation.

Charley We have to leave now. J.J. has to study for a test tomorrow.

Steve _____

J.J. So are we. We had a good time.

Stacy _____

J.J. It was nice meeting you, too, Stacy.

Steve _____

Charley Good night. . . . Oh, I almost forgot. I'm having some people over for dinner tomorrow night. Would you like to come?

Stacy _____

Charley How about you, Steve?

Steve _____

J.J. Well, I hope you both can come. Bye. (*Charley and J.J. walk away.*)

Stacy So, how do you know Charley?

Steve _____

40.

SURVEY: Why do people go back to school?

Our survey this week asks people why they continue their education, sometimes years after they have completed high school or graduated from college. Answers unanimously suggest that the changing workplace and job security are key factors.

Henry Lopez   High School Employment Counselor
At one time, taking a class or two after school or after work depended on a person's personal motivation or interest. Today we see a change in purpose. It seems that more and more people are going back to school because they've lost a job or for job security. A lot of people hate the idea of two additional years—or more—of school, but what are they going to do? They want to get ahead—and stay ahead. I tell students when they walk out the door that they are not finished with their education.

Ann Lin   Nurse
I'm not really worried about my job. Almost everybody in the medical profession is safe these days. But I do worry about keeping up-to-date and about getting a promotion. So I take a class once in a while to keep myself informed of new medical developments and to add new skills to my résumé. It's very important. I think people in general need to continue their education to stay employed.

Jason Waldbaum   College Student
I go to a community college—you know, a two-year program—and I'm studying computer technology. I think it's important for everybody to get training, especially in computers. As for me, I'd like to be a systems analyst. But already I feel the need for an additional two years of classes at a four-year university. Then I'll have a B.A. and it will look better on my résumé. I think there is a lot of competition in the workplace, and I want to be ready.

Gloria Graham   Retiree
I've never considered going back to school. I used to work, but I'm retired now, so I don't have to worry about staying on top of things. But I guess if I had to do it again, I'd go find a place where I could get some computer training. We're coming into a technological age—well, we are already there, aren't we?—and if you don't adapt, you'll be left behind. From what I read, the most jobs seem to be available in health care and computers. I'd try to get one of those.

Grant Tilton   Unemployed Airline Mechanic
I lost my job two years ago, and I couldn't find anything else in that field. I needed to do something because I have a family to support. So I decided the only way to be qualified for a different job was to go back to school—in my case, in computer technology. That's what I tell everybody. It's not easy and it's expensive, but I don't have much choice.

Kristine Olson   Dean, California Community College
We see a lot of changes in the job market and, consequently, in people's attitudes about education. Many jobs are changing or no longer exist because companies are rethinking the way they do business. They have automated their factories and do not need many of their current employees. The key is training—or retraining, actually—to find a job in a new area. Anything in the medical profession is hot—or in computers.

1. Read the survey. Then scan the survey and find:

a. two reasons people consider going back to school.
b. two areas that are hot in the job market.

2. Discuss this question.

How do people in your country compare to the interviewees above? In other words, are they worried about losing or keeping their jobs, and do they consider it important to continue their education?

Review of units 5-7

 1 ▶ Complete the weekend weather report with comparisons—. . .er (*than*), more/less . . . (*than*)—and the words in parentheses.
▶ Listen to check your work.
▶ Ask a classmate what the weather is going to be like this weekend.

Today's going to be _nicer than_ (nice) it was yesterday. It will be _less_____ (cloudy), so you can look forward to a clear sky. It will also be _sunnier_____ (sunny) and _warmer_____ (warm). And, of course, the beaches will be _____ (crowded) yesterday now that the weather is clearing up. Fortunately, for those people who are here on vacation, the weather forecast for next week is even _____ (good) the forecast for this weekend. For a _____ (complete) report, please tune in tonight for the six o'clock news.

2 ▶ It's Saturday and the weather is going to be good today, so Nicole and her boyfriend Randy are making plans. Complete Randy's part of the conversation.
▶ Act out a similar conversation with a partner.

Randy _I've got an idea for Saturday weekend. Let's go to a park._
Nicole Why don't we go to the beach instead? I like the beach better than the park.
Randy _Well,_____
Nicole By the way, what's the weather going to be like?
Randy _____
Nicole Good. Because I don't like the beach when it's windy or cool.
Randy _____
Nicole Yes. And we should also take something to drink. Everything is more expensive at those places on the beach.
Randy _____
Nicole Say, I have an idea. Why don't I invite my new neighbor, Gina, to go with us?
Randy _____
Nicole She's a lot of fun, and she has a great sense of humor.

3 ▶ Nicole and Gina live in the same apartment building. Compare their apartments using *just as . . . as* and *not as . . . as*.

Nicole's apartment	Gina's apartment
big enough for two people	big enough for one person
kitchen—7 feet by 8 feet	kitchen—7 feet by 8 feet
living room—12 feet by 18 feet	living room—11 feet by 13 feet
bedroom—12 feet by 14 feet	bedroom—12 feet by 14 feet
very sunny	not very sunny
quiet neighbors	noisy neighbors
rent—$600 a month	rent—$450 a month

4 ▶ Nicole and Randy are driving to the beach. Listen to their conversation. Then choose the picture of Gina.

1   2

5 ▶ Nicole and Randy see an accident on the way to the beach, and they stop to help. Complete the police officer's part of the conversation.
  ▶ Imagine you have just seen an accident. Have a similar conversation with a partner.

Police officer _____
   Nicole A car ran into that woman on the motorcycle. The car went right through a red light.
Police officer _____
   Nicole It was an old car. I don't know what kind.
Police officer _____
   Nicole Red.
Police officer _____
   Nicole Yes. It was KLJ 88B.

6 ▶ Randy is talking to the woman with the motorcycle. Put the lines of the conversation in order.
  ▶ Listen to check your work.

___ Yes. I guess I can.
___ Are you all right?
___ Well, I'm sorry that you wrecked your motorcycle, but I'm glad you didn't get hurt.
___ Yes, I'm fine. But look at my motorcycle.
___ You can always fix your motorcycle.
___ Don't mention it.
___ So am I. Anyway, I'll be O.K. Thanks for your help.

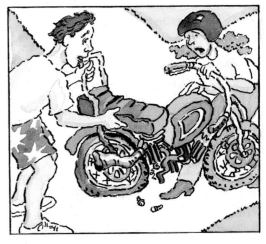

7 ▶ Randy and Nicole are at the beach. Complete the conversation with tag questions.
  ▶ Work with a partner. Act out the conversation, answering the questions with information about a third student.

Nicole She's a student at our school, _____?
Randy _____ .
Nicole She's not from here originally though, _____?
Randy _____ .
Nicole You know her name, _____?
Randy _____ .
Nicole She doesn't go to school full time, _____?
Randy _____ .

8 ► Imagine you are at the beach with some friends. Choose one of the questions below and start a conversation with a friend. Then continue the conversation, responding to your friend's answer.

Who wants a soda?
Where do you go to school?
What are you doing tonight?
You're (name of another student), aren't you?
So, how do you know (name of another student)?

Where are you from originally?
Have you ever had an accident?
Do you speak another language—besides
  your native language and English?
May I borrow your sunglasses?

9 ► When Randy and Nicole get home from the beach, they find Gina sitting on the steps of the apartment building. Complete their conversation.

► Imagine you lost something. Have a similar conversation with a partner.

Gina Oh, you're back. Thank goodness.
Nicole _____
Gina I lost my handbag, and my wallet and apartment key were in it.
Randy _____
Gina May I use your phone? I want to call the police.
Nicole _____
Gina Thanks.
Randy _____
Gina No, I don't. I lost all my identification too. But I can describe everything that's in my handbag, so I'm sure the police will give it back—if they have it.
Nicole _____
Gina So do I. Say, did you hear about the bank robbery at the First National Bank?
Nicole _____
Gina Here. You can read about it. I'm finished with the paper.

10A ► Student A follows the instructions below.
Student B follows the instructions on page 80.

Student A Read the newspaper articles below.
Ask your partner questions about the robbery
to fill in the blanks.
Then answer your
partner's questions
about the fire.

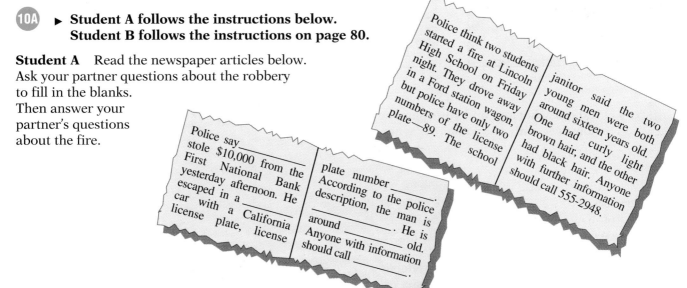

Police say _____ stole $10,000 from the First National Bank yesterday afternoon. He escaped in a _____ car with a California license plate, license plate number _____. According to the police description, the man is around _____. He is _____ old. Anyone with information should call _____.

Police think two students started a fire at Lincoln High School on Friday night. They drove away in a Ford station wagon, but police have only two numbers of the license plate—89. The school janitor said the two young men were both around sixteen years old. One had curly light brown hair, and the other had black hair. Anyone with further information should call 555-2948.

11 ► Play these roles.

Student A You think you'll have some people over for dinner on Saturday. Find out what B is doing this weekend and invite B to come. When B offers to bring something to drink or eat, tell B that you have everything you need.

Student B You have no plans this weekend, so you accept A's invitation. Ask if you can bring anything. Also, find out what time you should be there.

10B ▸ **Student B follows the instructions below.**
▸ **Student A follows the instructions on page 79.**

Student B Read the newspaper articles below.
Answer your partner's
questions about the
robbery. Then ask
your partner questions
about the fire to fill
in the blanks.

Police say a young man
stole $10,000 from the
First National Bank
yesterday afternoon. He
escaped in a red sports
car with a California
license plate, license
plate number FP 256.

According to the police
description, the man is
very tall with long blond
hair. He is around twenty
years old. Anyone with
information should call
555-3468.

12 ▸ **Gina is having dinner with Nicole
and Randy. Listen to the conversation and
check (√) the things Gina and Nicole have in common.**

13 ▸ **Find out what you and your partner have in common. Use
rejoinders with *so* and *neither* when appropriate.**

A *Do you like to rollerblade?*
B *Yes, I do. Do you?*
A *I don't know how. Do you like to swim?*
B *Yes, I do.*
A *So do I.*

14 ▸ **Gina is leaving and thanking Nicole
for dinner. Complete Gina's part of
the conversation.**
▸ **Act out a similar conversation with
a partner.**

Nicole You're not leaving already, are you?
Gina _____
Nicole Well, I'm glad you could come.
Gina _____

15 ▸ **Answer the questions with your
own information.**

1. You're at the end of the book. Do you think
   you'll take another English course?
2. Which course will you probably take?
3. Are your classmates planning to take the
   next course?
4. What are you going to do during the break—
   before the next class begins?

VOCABULARY LIST

The list includes both productive and receptive words introduced in Student Book 2B. Productive words are those which students use actively in interaction exercises. Receptive words are those which appear only in opening conversations, comprehension dialogues, readings, and instructions, and which students need only understand. Countries, languages, and nationalities are given in a separate list. The following abbreviations are used to identify words: V = verb, N = noun, ADJ = adjective, ADV = adverb, CONJ = conjunction, INTERJ = interjection, PR = pronoun, PREP = preposition, PAST PART. = past participle, COMP = comparative, SUPER = superlative, R = receptive. Page numbers indicate the first appearance of a word.

A

a great deal of 66 R
a lot 1
ABS (anti-lock brake system) 66 R
absolutely 12
acceptable 23
accident 13
accommodation(s) 51 R
account (= story) 22 R
across 9
act (V) 7
acting (N) 7
ad (= advertisement) 10
adapt 76 R
addition 66 R
advertising (department) 39
afraid 64
after all 2
age 76 R
ago 17
air bag 66 R
air conditioner 42 R
air conditioning 66 R
airplane 5 R
album 56 R
all right 14
all the way 22 R
already 28
alternative 47 R
amazing 42 R
ambulance 13
among 56 R
analyst 76 R
angry 4
ant 19
anti-lock 66 R
anxious 40
anybody 6
anyone 6
anyway 54
anywhere 1
application 35
apply 39 R
appreciate 71
area 14
as (CONJ, = when) 22 R
as . . . as 47
as soon as 5
ask 24
assistance 61 R
astronaut 42 R

at all 1
at first 3 R
at least 20
at once (= at the same time) 42 R
ate (PAST of eat) 19
attend 26 R
attention 12 R
attitude 76 R
author 32 R
automate 76 R
automated 66 R
automatic 42 R
automobile 5 R
avalanche 22 R
away (ADV) 9

B

B.A. 76 R
back (ADV) 2
back (N) 16
back (V) 62
back and forth 42 R
background 32 R
badly 51 R
bald 53
band 54
bandage 16
barbecue 67
bath 12 R
battery 66 R
be prepared 61 R
be supposed to 47
beard 53
because 3
been (PAST PART. of be) 23
belief 12 R
best-selling 56 R
better (COMP of good) 47
biking (go biking) 13
bill (dollar bill) 29
billion 42 R
bit (PAST of bite) 16
blanket 22 R
blond 53
blues (music) 56 R
bookseller 24
bored 4
born (to be born) 24
bottom 22 R
bought (PAST of buy) 10

boyfriend 70
brake(s) 57
brave 22 R
break (N) 11
break (V) 17
brief 17 R
broke (PAST of break) 13
broken (ADJ) 14
brought (PAST of bring) 10
brush (off) 22 R
building 43
burn (V) 16
business 11
busy 20
buyer 66 R
by the way 20

C

call (V) (on a phone) 9
call (V) (= shout) 22 R
calm 14
camping (go camping) 13
card 14
care (for) (V) 54
care (take care of) 21
careful 57
carriage 66 R
cash 29
cast (for a broken leg, etc.) 16
catch (V) 51 R
caught (PAST of catch) 51 R
CD (= compact disc) 24
celebrate 43
central 66 R
challenging 22 R
change (V) 44
charge (V) 29
cheap 37
check (bank check) 4
checklist 39 R
chemical 66 R
chemistry 54
chose (PAST of choose) 24
church 56 R
cleaner (N) 69
clear (ADJ) 77
clear (up) (V) 52
climb (V) 22 R

climber 22 R
climbing (N) 22 R
close (ADJ) 2 R
clothes 44
cloud 22 R
coach (N & V) 74
coffee shop 24
coincidence 69
collect (V) 26 R
collector 26 R
college 24
column 12 R
come on 3
come over 55 R
communication 42 R
companion 22 R
comparison 47 R
complete (ADJ) 77
concert 7
condition 66 R
conductor 30
confidence 12
confidential 39 R
congratulate 74
Congratulations! 74
consequently 66 R
continuation 27 R
continue 27 R
convenience 42 R
convenient 48
conversation 23
conversationalist 12
cost (V) 44
costume 7
could (V) 1
counselor 76 R
country (= nation) 23
course (in school) 73
critic 7 R
crowd (N) 51 R
crowded 77
curious 22 R
curly 47
current (ADJ) 66 R
customer 25
cut (V) 16

D

dance (N) 56 R
danger 22 R
dean (in a college) 76 R
decade 56 R

license plate 57
life 30
lifeguard 36
lift (V) 22 R
like (V) 1
like (PREP) 10
line (phone line) 20
list (V) 58
live (ADJ) 56 R
lock (V) 43
locksmith 44
look (N) 10
look forward to 77
look out 22 R
lose 53
loud 7
love (V) 7
luck 33
lucky 8
lyrics 24

M

made (PAST of *make*) 2
mail (N) 45
mail carrier 45
makeup 7
marry 30
master's degree 26 R
matter (What's the
   matter?) 10
meal 40
medical 14
member 22 R
memorial 38
men's room 39
mention (V) 57
met (PAST of *meet*) 48
meter 22 R
mid-term 11 R
middle 62
might (V) 6 R
miss (V) 20
mistake 1
model (N) 10
moment 30
monster 6 R
monument 38
mood 1
moody 53
moon 42 R
more 11
mother-in-law 18
motivation 76 R
motor 42 R
mountain 22 R
mountainside 22 R
move into 4
move to 9
music 7
musician 30
mustache 53
myself 67
mysterious 6 R

N

name (V) 23
nap (take a nap) 5 R
nation 56 R
national 15
near (V) 22 R
need (N) 12 R
negative 5 R
neglected 12
neither 20
nervous 1
never 9
news 1
night 4
nobody 6
noise 10
normal 51 R
nothing 2
notice (V) 23
nowhere 6

O

occasionally 12
of course 2
omit 63 R
on time 40
once in a while 76 R
opening (job opening)
   40 R
opera 30 R
optional 63 R
order (V) 23
ordinary 43 R
out of (PREP) 3
out of this world 6 R
outdoor (ADJ) 30 R
outgoing 12
outside 10
over (PREP) 36
over (= finished) 2
overheat 64
Ow! (INTERJ) 14
owe 23

P

paid (PAST of *pay*) 29
pajama 12 R
park (V) 10
parking (N) 51 R
part 15
part time 39
partly 32 R
party 1
pass (a test) 1
passenger 5 R
passport 57
perfect (V) 42 R
perform 30
performer 30
permission 57 R

personality 54
personnel 33
photograph (N) 29
physical education 74
picnic 70
pitch (V) 51 R
pitcher 51 R
planet 6 R
play (V) 3
player 20
pleasure 33
plus 44
police 43
police car 16
politely 23 R
pollution 66 R
popular 47
positive 5 R
possibility 5 R
poverty 56 R
prescription 5 R
pressure 40
pretty (ADV) 2
previous 56 R
prince 32 R
princess 32 R
problem 10
promote 56 R
promotion 76 R
prove 12 R
pull (V) 66 R
pull up 22 R
purchase (N) 29
put on 16

Q

qualification 39 R
qualified (ADJ) 76 R
queen 6 R
quick 42 R
quiet 47
quit (V) 73

R

radiator 64
radio 10
radio (V) 22 R
rainy 52
ran (PAST of *run*) 15
rap (music) 56 R
real 43
realize 42 R
recommendation 13 R
record (N) 56 R
recording 56 R
red light 57
refreshment 51 R
reggae (music) 56 R
register (V) 73
reject (V) 6 R
relaxed (ADJ) 12 R

relaxing (ADJ) 18
religious 22 R
remember 28
report (N) 58
reporter 35
request (V) 57 R
rescue (N) 22 R
rescuer 22 R
responsible 63
rest (N) 14
résumé (N) 76 R
rethink 76 R
retired (ADJ) 76 R
retiree 76 R
retraining 76 R
rhythm 56 R
ride (N) 64
right away 14
road 57
robbery 16
rock (= stone) 15
rock (music) 54
rock 'n' roll 56 R
rode (PAST of *ride*) 19
rollerblade (V) 80
romantic 46
roof 16
roommate 70
root(s) 56 R
rope 22 R
rough 20
run into 15
rush (N) 40

S

safe 76 R
safely 22 R
sang (PAST of *sing*) 32 R
satellite 42 R
scared (ADJ) 4
scene 57
scenery 7
scientific 42 R
search (for) 22 R
seat belt 63
security 76 R
seem 11
seen (PAST PART. of *see*)
   10
sell (V) 17
semester 36
sense (of humor) 48
sensor 66 R
service (N) 7
service (V) 44 R
settle down 30
sewing (N) 32 R
shelter 22 R
short 49
shot (= inoculation) 16
show (V) 7
shy 53
sign (V) 61

SUPPLEMENTARY VOCABULARY

IRREGULAR VERBS

Base form	Simple past	Past participle	Base form	Simple past	Past participle
be	was, were	been	lend	lent	lent
beat	beat	beaten	let	let	let
become	became	become	lie	lay	lain
begin	began	begun	lose	lost	lost
bend	bent	bent	make	made	made
bite	bit	bitten	mean	meant	meant
blow	blew	blown	meet	met	met
break	broke	broken	pay	paid	paid
bring	brought	brought	put	put	put
build	built	built	quit	quit	quit
buy	bought	bought	read	read [rɛd]	read [rɛd]
catch	caught	caught	ride	rode	ridden
choose	chose	chosen	ring	rang	rung
come	came	come	rise	rose	risen
cost	cost	cost	run	ran	run
cut	cut	cut	say	said	said
deal	dealt	dealt	see	saw	seen
dig	dug	dug	sell	sold	sold
do	did	done	send	sent	sent
draw	drew	drawn	set	set	set
drink	drank	drunk	shake	shook	shaken
drive	drove	driven	shoot	shot	shot
eat	ate	eaten	shut	shut	shut
fall	fell	fallen	sing	sang	sung
feed	fed	fed	sit	sat	sat
feel	felt	felt	sleep	slept	slept
fight	fought	fought	slide	slid	slid
find	found	found	speak	spoke	spoken
fit	fit	fit	spend	spent	spent
fly	flew	flown	stand	stood	stood
forget	forgot	forgotten	steal	stole	stolen
get	got	gotten	stick	stuck	stuck
give	gave	given	strike	struck	struck
go	went	gone	sweep	swept	swept
grow	grew	grown	swim	swam	swum
have	had	had	swing	swung	swung
hear	heard	heard	take	took	taken
hide	hid	hidden	teach	taught	taught
hit	hit	hit	tear	tore	torn
hold	held	held	tell	told	told
hurt	hurt	hurt	think	thought	thought
keep	kept	kept	throw	threw	thrown
know	knew	known	understand	understood	understood
lay	laid	laid	wear	wore	worn
lead	led	led	win	won	won
leave	left	left	write	wrote	written

SOME COUNTRIES AND NATIONALITIES

Country	Nationality	Country	Nationality
Algeria	Algerian	Kuwait	Kuwaiti
Argentina	Argentine	Korea	Korean
Afghanistan	Afghan	Laos	Laotian
Australia	Australian	Lebanon	Lebanese
Austria	Austrian	Lithuania	Lithuanian
Bolivia	Bolivian	Malaysia	Malaysian
Brazil	Brazilian	Mexico	Mexican
Bulgaria	Bulgarian	Mongolia	Mongolian
Canada	Canadian	Morocco	Moroccan
Chad	Chadian	Nepal	Nepalese
Chile	Chilean	Nicaragua	Nicaraguan
China	Chinese	Nigeria	Nigerian
Colombia	Colombian	Norway	Norwegian
Costa Rica	Costa Rican	Pakistan	Pakistani
Cuba	Cuban	Paraguay	Paraguayan
Czechoslovakia	Czech	Peru	Peruvian
Ecuador	Ecuadorian	Panama	Panamanian
Egypt	Egyptian	Poland	Polish
Ethiopia	Ethiopian	Portugal	Portuguese
Finland	Finnish	Saudi Arabia	Saudi
France	French	Spain	Spanish
Gambia	Gambian	Somalia	Somalian
Germany	German	Sweden	Swedish
Guyana	Guyanese	Switzerland	Swiss
Ghana	Ghanan	Syria	Syrian
Greece	Greek	Thailand	Thai
Guatemala	Guatemalan	The Dominican Republic	Dominican
Haiti	Haitian		
Honduras	Honduran	The Netherlands	Dutch
Hungary	Hungarian	The Philippines	Filipino
India	Indian	The United Kingdom	British
Indonesia	Indonesian	The United States of America	American
Iran	Iranian		
Iraq	Iraqi	Tunisia	Tunisian
Ireland	Irish	Turkey	Turkish
Israel	Israeli	Venezuela	Venezuelan
Italy	Italian	Vietnam	Vietnamese
Japan	Japanese	Yugoslavia	Yugoslavian
Jordan	Jordanian	Zaire	Zairian
Kenya	Kenyan	Zambia	Zambian

SOME LANGUAGES

Arabic	French	Mandarin	Swahili
Bengali	German	Mongolian	Swedish
Cantonese	Greek	Nahuatl	Tagalog
Czech	Hausa	Norwegian	Tamil
Danish	Hebrew	Polish	Thai
Dutch	Hindi	Portuguese	Turkish
English	Hungarian	Quechua	Urdu
Estonian	Italian	Romanian	Vietnamese
Farsi	Japanese	Russian	Zulu
Finnish	Korean	Spanish	